BHOTIA TRIBALS OF INDIA

Dynamics of Economic
Transformation

Bhotia Tribals of India

Dynamics of Economic Transformtion

R.R. PRASAD

GYAN PUBLISHING HOUSE
New Delhi - 110002

Bhotia Tribals of India
Dynamics of Economic Transformation

ISBN : 978-81-212-0251-0

Published, 2016

Published in India by

Gyan Publishing House
5, Ansari Road
Daryaganj, New Delhi-110002
Phone: 9811692060
E-mail: books@gyanbooks.com
Webside: gyanbooks.com

Printed at: G. Print Process, Delhi.

DEDICATED

TO

THE SACRED MEMORY

OF MY FATHER

LATE SACHCHIDANAND PRASAD

Preface

This study seeks to understand the dynamics of economic transformation and cultural adaptation among the Bhotia tribals. 'Bhotia' is a generic term used to designate several socially unrelated groups of Indo-Tibetan borderland in the Himalayan and trans-Himalayan regions. In the eastern Himalayas the term includes groups of people living in the Nepalese-Tibetan border areas, the Tibetans staying in the vicinity of Darjeeling and the inhabitants of Bhutan. In the Central Himalayan regions of Garhwal and Kumaon the northern non-Tibetan highlanders are referred to by this generic term. Bhotia is an exclusive community, different both from the Hindus and the Tibetans. Traditionally the Bhotias were connected with trade and from times immemorial they carried it on between India and Tibet. Trade with Tibet has been the mainstay of the Bhotia economy. The impact of the physiographic environment and trade with Tibet had been so great on the Bhotias' socio-cultural life that they had sought to seasonal nomadism which forced them to build a distinct socio-economic structure. The trans-Himalayan trade of the Bhotias had influence not only on their day-to-day activity but it also determined and shaped their entire course of socio-cultural life. But, due to extraneous factor, the Indo-Tibetan trade of the Bhotias was suddenly disrupted. This sudden disruption of the Indo-Tibetan trade, which was the mainstay of Bhotias' economy, and an adjunct to their socio-cultural life forced them to seek alternative sources of livelihood and modify the socio-cultural life in conformity with the changed environment. How the Bhotias have reacted to this sudden gust of change in the core of their economic system, and how far they have been able to adapt themselves to the changed socio-economic situation, is the central theme of this study.

The study has been spread over a very large and wide compass, beginning from the emergence of trading activities of the Bhotias, its impact on their socio-cultural life, and then finally to the consequences of decline in trade, and the adaptive processes geared to cope with it. This has been done to understand the magnitude and process of change activised by the influence of exogenous factor on the economic system which has its effect on the web of the interacting pattern of social, religious, political system and subsistence strategies. A longer spread of time has provided a more meaningful and analytical perspective. Thus, the study which covers a vast period of growth and development of Bhotia society is calculated to provide a better insight into the dynamics of change in tribal community and the various socio-cultural processes which facilitate a community in adapting to such changes.

In undertaking this study I have received assistance from a number of individuals and organizations. While it is difficult to acknowledge all of them individually, I would like to acknowledge my profound gratefulness to the following persons who have been particularly helpful in this work.

At the outset I acknowledge my sincere senseof gratitude to Prof. S.C. Tiwari, Head, Department of Anthropology, Delhi University, Delhi for allowing me to use the data collected from the U.G.C. sponsored research project "Socio-biological study of the three endogamous ethnic groups of Indo-Nepal and Indo-Tibetan Borders" in which I worked as Junior Research Fellow for three years, for my doctoral dissertation. I am also very thankful to Dr. J.S. Bhandari, Reader, Department of Anthropology, Delhi University for his valuable guidance during the project work. I was greatly facilitated in my work by my colleagues S/Shri A.K. Kapoor, R.N. Katayayan, and Naresh Vaid. I am grateful to them.

I also acknowledge my deep and sincere sense of gratitude to my teacher and supervisor Dr. V.S. Upadhyay, Reader, Department of Anthropology, Ranchi University for helping me in writing my doctoral dissertation. I must also extend my sincere thanks to my teacher, mentor and guide Late Prof. L.P. Vidyarthi for encouraging me to undertake this research study. I shall be failing in my duty if I do not extend my thanks to my field informants S/Shri Guman Singh Panchpal, Govind Singh Pangtey, Bhopal Singh Pangtey and many other Bhotia prople. I cannot forget to record my deep sense of reverence and love for my parents and brothers and sisters who have constantly encouraged me to successfully complete this work.

Last, but not the least, I am thankful to Shri J.N. Sahay for typing out the manuscript.

R.R. PRASAD

Contents

List of Tables

List of Maps

1

Introduction

PERSPECTIVE

No society is static. It is difficult to think of an area of society that is untouched by the process of change. Change is inevitable. There are forces at work in every society leading to the alteration and modification in the patterned system through which a group functions; either in its internal life or in reference to external realities. In the course of development the socio-cultural system of every society incessantly dies and incessantly resurrects and revives itself. Sorokin (1941) says, "death and resurrection is a perennial uniformity of the life of a culture as long as it lives." To be in an incessant flux, as Heraclitus said, is their destiny. Although change lies implicit in the natural environment, there are, at the same time, certain forces and rhythms operative in the environment and in the group which effect working adjustments and permit the community to survive. It is generally assumed that as a culture experiences its environment, the behaviour system will be shaped by that experience. Therefore, change in the environment, either in its element or whole, will lead to a corresponding change in the behaviour system of the environed unit—be it an individual, a group, or a community. The behaviour of the environed unit, in order to cope successfully with the consequences of the change in the environment, must be steered in such a fashion that it reduces the conflict with the environment. To make the behaviour adaptable to the changed environment, the environed unit is required to reallocate its resources and reorientate the course of socio-cultural life so as to effect a harmonious and congruous relationship with the changed environment.

What are the causes and dimensions of change in the socio-cultural system ? How different societies react and adapt to the changes in their environment? These are some of the questions which pose challange to most social scientists. An investigation into these issues is of vital importance because it brings home the empirical grounds for understanding the causes of change in the socio-cultural system, and knowing the coping mechanism or strategic actions of the group involved in adaptation to a novelty resulting in the socio-cultural change.

The present treatise is essentially an attempt in the sphere of studying the dynamics of change and cultural adaptation. Ryan (1969) says, "change occurs only when novelty alters the patterned system through which a group functions". Thus, any study on change must identify first the novelty or the factor which is responsible for bringing alterations and modifications in the patterned system. In this study the community chosen is of the BHOTIAS and the novelty or the factor which is responsible for effecting change in their socio-cultural system, is the disruption of their Indo-Tibetan trade.

Bhotia is a generic term used to designate several socially unrelated groups of Indo-Tibetan borderland in the Himalayan and trans-Himalayan regions. In the Eastern Himalayas the term includes group of people living in the Nepalese-Tibetan border areas, the Tibetans staying in the vicinity of Darjeeling and the inhabitants of Bhutan. In the Central Himalayan regions of Garhwal and Kumaon the northern non-Tibetan highlanders are referred to by this generic term while the plains-men hardly make any distinction as they refer to the

Tibetans too as 'Bhotia' (Das, 1982). In fact, the term Bhotia is applied traditionally to all peoples along the interface from the Sultej to Bhutan associated with the now disappearing Indo-Tibetan trade, but so dispersed and varied that the term tends to become somewhat randomly applied (Brown, 1987).

Bhotia is the term applied to the people associated with the area called "Bhot" especially in the Central Himalayan area. It seems that a popularization of the term is in some way connected to British expansion from Bengal past Nepal to the Western Himalayan area in the 18th and 19th centuries A.D. The earliest British references to the "Booteas" associated them with Bhutan. Thus concerning the British-Bhutan war, the British records speak of an "invasion of Cooch Behar" by the Booteas (Bhutanese) in 1772. In fact during the time of Hastings when contacts were first made by the British with Tibet proper, Bhutan and Tibet were conceptualized together as "Boutan',, and the inhabitants called "Boutans" or "Booteas" (cf. e.g. on Hastings and Bogle in Markham, 1879). As British expansion pushed into the Himalayan regions of modern Uttar Pradesh, the administrators were confronted once again with a problem. This time the issue was further confused by the term "Hundes" which referred to Western Tibet (mNga-ris) and forced the administrators to differentiate the Bhot of British territory from the Hundes of Tibet. R. Strachey (1851: 85) follows Atkinson's interpretation of Hundes as the "country of Huns" as opposed to "Undes" (wool-country) or even "Huindes" (snow-country), which is Trail's interpretation and probably the most sensible. It may be noted that Trail in an "enclosure" to the Board of Revenue of the Ceded and Conquered Provinces, 25th July, 1817 refers to Western Tibet as "Northern Bhote" in speaking of the Bhotia trade system in general (No. 13A in Board of Revenue 1817). It is probably quite true as D.N. Majumdar once noted:

> "The part of the country inhabited by the Bhotiyas, is known in Kumaon as Bhot while the Kumaonese call Tibet as Hundesh and the Tibetans are known to them as the Huniyas. The Bhotias also use the same appellation for

the Tibetans and for the country of the Tibetans, they use Hundesh. According to popular belief, the words Bhot and Bhotiya were mainly popularized by the British administration, due probably to the cultural similarity with the people of Sikkim and Bhutan states..." (1949: II-III)

The generality of the term even when used today can be exemplified by Bagchi who, in describing some characteristics of the eastern Himalayan area, refers to certain groups of Nepal. Bhutan and even to some Tibetans as the "Bhutias" (1977:366). Sastry interprets this identity more precisely in noting the generic character of the name as applicable to certain non-Tibetan peoples of the border region who have traditionally been practitiners of the trade between India and Tibet. (1975: 19)

The border regions of Kumaon and Garhwal Himalayas of India are inhabited by a number of semi-nomadic groups who, when referred to collectively, are known by the generic term Bhotia. Bhotia is an exclusive community, different both from the Hindus and the Tibetans. Although there are Bhotias in Nepal, Sikkim, Bhutan and Tibet also, the present study is primarily concerned with the Bhotias of Kumaon and Garhwal Himalayas. Traditionally the Bhotias were connected with trade and from times immemorial they have carried it on between India and Tibet. Trade has been the mainstay of the Bhotia economy. They used to supply commodities obtained from Tibet to the warm, fertile valleys down south. Traditionally the articles which Bhotias used to sell in the Tibet were rice, wheat, sugar, gur, tobacco, copper, gold, iron, hardware, silver and Indian cotton piecegoods, cigarettes, matches, etc. From Tibet they used to bring salt, gold dust, borax, wool, furs, yak-tails, goats and sheeps, mules, etc. The impact of the physiographic environment and trade with Tibet had been so great on the Bhotias' socio-cultural life that they had sought to seasonal nomadism which forced them to build a distinct socio-economic structure. The trans-Himalayan trade of the Bhotias had not only influence on their day to day activity but it also determined and shaped their entire course of socio-cultural life. But, due to extraneous factor i.e., the Sino-Indian border conflict of 1962, the Indo-Tibetan trade of the Bhotias was suddenly disrupted. This sudden disruption of the Indo-Tibetan trade, which was the mainstay of Bhotias' economy and an adjunct to their socio-cultural life, forced them to seek alternative sources of livelihood and modify the socio-cultural life in conformity with the changed environment. How the Bhotias have reacted to this sudden gust of change in the core of their economic system, and how far they have been able to adapt themselves to the changed socio-economic situation, is the central theme of this study.

The study has been spread over a very large and wide compass, beginning from the emergence of trading activities of the Bhotias, its impact on their socio-culturul life, and then finally to the consequences of decline in trade, and the adaptive processes geared to cope with it. This has been done to understand the magnitude and process of change activised by the influence of exogenous factor on the economic system which has its effect on the web of the interacting pattern of social, religious, political system and subsistence strategies. A longer spread of time has provided a more meaningful and analytical perspective. Thus, the study which covers a vast period of growth and development of Bhotia society, is calculated to provide a better insight in the dynamics of change in a community towards a vital objective of tribal development.

The problem of the present research is worded as under:

BHOTIA TRIBALS OF INDIA :
Dynamics of Economic Transformation

In order to clarify the problem, it is necessary to define the important terms used in the statement of the problem of research. Sometimes the meaning of a single term may be expressed in various shades which are relevant to the aims and objectives of the researcher. Hence, it would not be out of place to list the various shades of meaning of a single term which are relevant to the present study.

The term '*Dynamics*' refers to the study of:

(a) interrelationship between motion and the forces effecting motion, and

(b) the physical or moral forces that produce motion and change in any field or system.

The term '*Economic*' refers to the sum total of practices or activities developed by a community to obtain means of livelihood. Though there may be a number of activities and practices designed to accrue income, in the present study, the term 'economic' refers largely to the primary source of income or livelihood.

The term '*Transformation*', in the present context, denotes or relates to:

(a) movement from one state of organisational affairs to another state;

(b) marked change in the form or appearance of the erstwhile organisational affairs;

(c) a change in the nature and function, or condition of the organisation.

'*Cultural Adaptation*' refers to the coping mechanisms that humans display in adjusting to both short-term fluctuations and long-term changes in the interplay of their socio-cultural components or structure of their environment.

'*Bhotia*' is a generic term which refers to that bulk of population who inhabit the borderlands of Kumaon and Garhwal, and speak the Tibeto-Burman branch of dialect. The Bhotias of Kumaon and Garhwal are divided into five endogamous groups such as *Johari*, *Shauka*, *Tolcha*, *Marcha* and *Jad* Bhotias. These Bhotia groups are concentrated in four districts namely, Almora, Pithoragarh, Chamoli, and Uttarkashi of the Indian State of Uttar Pradesh. The present study is concerned with that group of Bhotias who are known as *Johari Bhotias* and are concentrated in the Johar valley of Munsiari tehsil in the Pithoragarh District of Kumaon Division.

IMPORTANCE OF THE STUDY

Tribals living in isolation develop their own customs and socio-economic institutions which are the results of hundreds of years of gradual adaptation to their environment. So any abrupt, unplanned or unprecedented change in their environment disturbs that equilibrium and causes much discomfort to the tribal folk. This may even lead to their degeneration, despondency or loss of initiative.

The study of dynamics of change and socio-cultural adaptation in the Bhotia society presupposes many significant and important points which encompass this research work. The Bhotias inhabit an isolated valley in the border regions of the Central Himalayas. To survive and prosper in this mountanious terrain which is mostly arid and snow-bound for almost half of the year, nearly requires exceptional accommodation skill and competence to blend with the local environment. The Bhotias not only survived in such a desolate and relatively isolated environment but also developed a viable relationship with their environment. Hence, it is quite significant to know how Bhotias were able to develop a viable relationship with such an inhospitable and rugged terrain of their environment. The importance of such a study lies in the sense that it leads to an appreciation of the varieties of adaptation that have enabled these people to survive in their difficult environment. In other words, the present study greatly helps in understanding the relationship between habitat, economy, and society over a vast period of time.

The other important aspect of this study is to develop an insight into trading methods of the Bhotias, a system which was based on barter, mutual understanding and faith between the Bhotias and the Tibetans, and the *Pahari* people. An analysis of this trading system is of great significance because it helps to understand the systems of trade relations that in other parts of the world belong to the distant past. Emphasising the importance of the Bhotia trading methods Prof. Haimendorf (1975) says that, "it is a way of life which involves a high degree of mobility, mercantile skills and the enterprenurial courage to risk capital may thus be soon a thing of the past, and this places the anthropologist, still able to observe the functioning of the trans-Himalayan barter trade in all its detail, under the urgent obligation to record a type of commerce soon to disappear from the face of the earth". Prof. Haimendorf's this remark is based on his observations on the Bhotias of Nepal who are still carrying out their trade, though in a rudimentary form, with Tibet. But such a trade system has already been officially stopped for the Bhotias of Indian nationality. Thus, under such circumstances, the study of the trading methods, as developed by Bhotias, becomes all the more important and significant.

The study of Bhotia society in its contemporary situation is again important for it stresses the importance of cultural flexibility as an adaptive strategy of a community. Further, by studying the impact of change in the economic system on the socio-cultural life of the people, one understands the network of relationship between the subsistence techniques and social organisation.

However, the most important aspect of this study is to identify the social problems of the Bhotia society which have emerged or cropped up in their society due to the sudden gust of change in the economic system and socio-cultural elements. Ogburn (1966) says that, "when culture begins to change, the modifications do not occur evenly in all parts of the social heritage. Some parts change faster then others. When the different parts are interrelated, the varying rates of change produce a strain between the unequally moving parts. Therefore, to lessen the strain of social problem due to unequal rates of change the most practical method of effecting a better integration between the two parts is to make some adjustment in the part that is lagging". The importance of the present study lies in the fact that, in the light of the research work and subsequent findings, the lagging parts of the Bhotias' culture will be identified and the development strategies will also be suggested. Such development strategies will naturally be suggested by taking into consideration the local conditions, and thus help the administrative and developmental agencies to provide the needed help and ensure community animation.

SCOPE AND LIMITATION

The scope of the present research is limited to the study of Bhotia society in its contemporary situation. The study covers only the Bhotias of Johar valley who are known as Johari Bhotias and not the other Bhotia groups living in the same surrounding areas and beyond. However, in studying the adaptive processes of the Johari Bhotias, the other Bhotia groups like Jad, Tolcha, Marcha, and Shauka will incidentally be touched upon for the sake of comparison.

The present study has certain limitations too. They are deemed to be unavoidable. In a changing situation a diachronic treatment of the material is essential for an understanding of the processes involved, but the application of such treatment is limited by the availability of information covering a long time-span. The process of change could be traced only by depending on the memory of men who have seen the old order and are conscious of the fact that they are living in a period of transition likely to alter or revolutionize the whole life style. Ogburn (1966) has rightly remarked that, "degree of adjustment between the two variables before, between and after the dates of change is not easy to prove". Thus, for a proper understanding of the changing socio-economic conditions of the Bhotia people, one has to take the temporal factor into consideration i.e., the range of period which marked the phase of cultural stability and that from where the Bhotias' social economy perceptibly started to disintegrate. This unavoidably demands the account of the old order and the new order of the Bhotia society. Here I shall present comparative material from between prior to 1962 and after 1962 which will serve to demonstrate the range of variations within the economic system of the Johari Bhotias.

The portion of study which deals with the old order of the Bhotia society is largely based on the facts gathered from the District Gazetteers, Settlement Reports, travelogues, and interview with the old people who have seen the old order. This could not be avoided as practically no published anthropological work dealing with the socio-cultural life of Bhotias is available. However, there are some works by the scholars of allied disciplines like Economics and Geography on the socio-cultural life of the Bhotias. S.D. Pant's "Social Economy of Himalayas" is by far the only book on the social economy of the hill people including Bhotias of U.P. But this too does not lead us far for it has not dealt the socio-cultural life of the Bhotias in detail. It rather gives a comprehensive account of all the Bhotia groups and thus providing only a sketchy account of the separate Bhotia groups on the basis of their territory and cultural practices.

The study is also focussed on the analysis of the social change that has taken place in the Bhotia society as a result of the sudden disruption of Bhotias' Indo-Tibetan trade which has been the main pillar of their economic system. The scope of the study is, therefore, limited to the change in the subunits of religion, social organisation, customs, norms, values, etc. activised by the change in the main unit i.e. economy of the Bhotia society.

The present study does not distinguish between the social and cultural change, because the emphasis on social and cultural change cuts across conventional distinctions between social and cultural, as they are both intrinsic to the conception of social system. Thus, culture change requires social factors as agents, and social change is likely to have cultural counterparts. The term 'culture', in the present work, thus, also includes social factors.

RESEARCH TECHNIQUES

Research techniques are the important avenues of collecting, classifying, analysing and interpreting the material and data collected from the field surveys. The present study has involved methods of anthropological and sociological repertory. As regards the material, the informations has been gathered from both the documentary and field sources through various techniques such as observation, interview, genealogy, schedules, photography, etc. The use of records, including archivial materials, has been quite helpful in this work.

Almost an year's field-work, at the successive periods, was done from January 1978 to December 1978. Some information were also collected by short visits in the closing months of the year 1979 to supplement the data and fill up the gaps.

The field observations were made from different angles, depending upon the situation : Sometimes as a participant, at other times as a non-participant observer. Likewise; controlled and uncontrolled observations simultaneously were found practicable. As aids to observation , notes and photographs were also taken. The interviews were conducted with males and females of different age-groups, on indivdual and group basis. In most of the interviews, notes were taken side by side and doubtful information were counterchecked. In the organization and analysis of the data collected, several steps were taken to be accurate. Screening was first done to delete unwanted materials. Through the editing operation, checks were made between the original blueprint or frame of the study and the data were collected. In classification, the categories in the proper settings were formed for presenting the data. Thus, the analysis or the creative part of research was done stepwise to draw systematic inferences in a sequential form. The results were finally translated into conceptual language, mainly in the light of the existing concepts and theories on which the study has been based.

SAMPLE

To give quantitative support to descriptive account, socio-economic surveys were carried out in 224 Bhotia families through schedules. These families represent the various stages of the Bhotia society which have assumed new form after the change in their socio-economic structure. These families are settled in the different villages of Johar valley. The selection of the Bhotia villages was done on the basis of their representativeness of the socio-cultural life, demographic characteristics, and settlement pattern. In this sample of Bhotia families, I have covered about 80 families who have abandoned their home village and have got settled down in different suburban and urban centres like Thal, Garur, Bageshwar, Didihat, Gwaldham, Almora, Pithoragarh and Haldwani. Besides this, families from the Bhotia villages of Malla Johar and Talla Johar were collected which consists of about 144 Bhotia families. The village of Malla Johar selected for study are Talla Dummer, Malla Dummer, Darkot, Daranthi, Ranthi, Suring, and those of the Talla Johar are Tejam and Timtia. Samples on the Bhotia families were collected on the basis of random sampling technique. However, the use of random sample was limited only in the big Bhotia villages. No random sampling was done in the small Bhotia villages.

HYPOTHESES

This study aims to test some of the hypotheses which are relevant to the dynamics of socio-cultural change and adaptation in tribal societies. Basing the study in the district of Central Himalayas where the Bhotia tribe inhabits, the following hypotheses have been envisaged by the investigator :

1. There always exists a disequilibrium tendency between a social system and its environment.
2. Any serious change in the important element or part of a socio-cultural system results in the simultaneous change in the correlated parts of the system.
3. Generation of new resources lead to potentially new level of organisational structures.
4. Behaviours which conform to the direction of change in the environment will be awarded and those which fail to conform will eventually face degeneration.
5. Every culture has inherent in its system a strategy of

adaptation through which people make effective use of their environment under different circumstances.

6. Man's social life is modified in adaptation to the demands and potentials inherent in his cultural equipment and related techniques.
7. Continuity and discontinuity with the pretransformation social system is maximised or minimized by the community's understanding of its environmental gradients.
8. No adaptation is permanent.

OBJECTIVES

The major objective of this research work is to study the Bhotia tribe in its contemporary situation. The Bhotia community has undergone a vicissitude of change due to very powerful factors which were mainly political but had a tremendous effect on their socio-cultural life. These changes have entirely altered the life style of the Bhotia community. From a non-sedentary trading community they have been forced to adapt to an entirely new way of life. Their social organisation, which developed and crystallized over centuries, had adapted itself to a particular environment and ecology which had also shaped their economic structure. But suddenly the economic structure, which may be regarded as the main pillar of the Bhotia society crumbled and along with the whole edifice of Bhotia life changed. A society that undergoes such a vertical change has to cope with a variety of problems. These problems are not merely economic, but primarily social and psychological. A tribe which is undergoing such a trauma and flux in its social life places the anthropologist under the urgent obligation to study the process of change and adaptive processes geared to cope with the new environmental conditions. To put it more specifically, the objectives of the present research work are :

1. To study the interrelationship of environment, subsistence techniques, and society.

2. To examine the social co-efficients of a trading or a commercial economy.
3. To develop an insight into the trading methods of the Bhotia.
4. To examine how does a change in important element or part of a society effect the other correlated elements and in what degree.
5. To enquire into the consequences of change in the economic structure of the Bhotia society and discover how far the Bhotias have been able to cope themselves with the new situation and also what have been their adaptive strategies.
6. To examine whether the pursuance of trade as a central economic activity produces certain social attitudes and arrangments, or people motivated by a specific outlook are more likely to achieve success in trading than communities conditioned by a diffeient ideology.
7. To what extent external factors or components act as a positive and negative agent in adapting the group to a changed environmental condition.
8. To suggest measure for development of the Bhotia community on the basis of my investigation into their socio-economic condition.

THEORETICAL FRAME OF REFERENCE

The analysis of socio-cultural change and adaptation in the Bhotia society is intended to be based on a theoretical frame of reference, developed with the help of the criteria usually accepted by the Sociologists and Social Anthropologists, as meaningful indices to observe and assess the nature of transformation and adaptive processes that take place in a society at different stages of its development. This study primarily embodies two aspects of socio-cultural phenomena-*change*, and *adaptation*. Hence, it is quite imperative to deal separately with the concepts discussing the theoretical aspects of these two phenomena and thus, finally develop a theoretical frame of reference for analysing change and adaptation in the Bhotia society.

SOCIO-CULTURAL CHANGE : A THEORETICAL ORIENTATION

Theories dealing with social and cultural change focus mainly on two aspects :

1. Why change occurs?
2. What is the direction of change?

So let us scan through the theories and propositions which account for these two pertinent questions on change.

Why does change take place in the sociocultural system? Where shall we look for the roots of change and how shall we interpret it? Shall we look for the causes, forces, or factors etc. leading to change? Ryan (1969) says, "social change occurs when the relationship among persons or groups are modified and, it always arises in reference to some established pattern in social relationship". Alvin Boskoff (quoted by Ryan), who hold more or less similar view says, "social change refers to the intelligible process in which we can discover significant alterations in the structure and functioning of determinate social systems". By significant alterations, Boskoff means, the variations that have novel consequences for the social system being studied. Emphasising the process of change Sorokin (1941) says, " not only socio-cultural phenomena, but all empirical phenomena, inorganic, organic, and socio-cultural are subject to change in the course of their empirical existence.

Sorokin (1941) has given three explanations for understanding the cause of socio-cultural change. The first explanation is the 'externalistic theory of change'. Such a theory looks for the reasons of change of any socio-cultural system in some variable (s) that lie outside the socio-cultural system. Broadly viewed, environmentalism is a theory and method of externalistic explanation of any change through environmental forces that lie outside but not within the unit studied. A further variety of the externalism is a wide current of 'reform' and 'reconstructive' movements which look for the roots of evil and for the potential cure of any social and cultural phenomenon in the institutions or external units under consideration. The second explanation is the 'immanent theory of cnange' which claim that culture changes by virtue of its own forces and propositions. There has been the third 'intermediary or integral' explanation to the cause of social change. It attempts to view change of any socio-cultural phenomenon as the result of combined external and internal forces. Emphasising the role of external forces Sorokin (1941) says, "external circumstances are neither necessary, nor permanent, nor universal cause of change of these systems. They are only auxiliary and intermittent reasons (causes) for change, sometimes favouring, sometimes disfavouring change, sometimes accelerating, sometimes slowing, once in a while catastrophically crushing the system".

Ryan (1969) broadly divides the scholarly interest of sociologists in the phenomenon of change into three categories :

1. analysis of dynamic and causal forces giving rise to social and cultural change;
2. analysis of the processes of change within social system; and
3. analysis of the transformation or evolution of social system, especially in regard to historical stages and trends in institutions and in society.

Theories dealing with the dynamic and causal forces of change posit 'prime movers' behind institutional and societal changes. Theories dealing with the dynamic force behind certain prime movers have two broad divisions—1. 'deterministic' and 2. 'particularistic'. The deterministic theory of change assumes the existence of direct cause and effect relationship in historic sequences. Similarly, the particularisitc theory assigns dynamic or causal significance to a single variable or to some closely related set of variables.

Robert E. Park (quoted by Ryan) believed that great cultural changes were due to confrontation of peoples and their cultures in which a revolution of society came about through the impact of the outsiders upon the society in question. Such invasions disorganize the society under attack, necessiating its reorganization.

Some catastrophies such as economic depression arise through the functioning of the internal social system. However, natural forces or actions of the other societies can create catastrophic conditions for societies normally well and efficiently integrated internally, ecologically and to outside group as well.

Charles P. Loomis (quoted by Ryan) and others have emphasised the frequency with which communities meet their disasters through substantial retention of their normal patterns of action. They further say that pre-existing patterns are especially prone to reassert themselves in the recovery and post-disaster stages. Discontinuity with the pre-disaster social system is maximized by catastrophies which permanently destroy the ecological balance of the society.

The 'structural—functional approach', set forth in the works of Talcott Parsons and his disciples (quoted by Eisenstadt: 1978), emphasises two causes of change in the social system: first, the disequilibrium tendencies that exist in the relationship between a social system and its environment; and second, the strain that exists between the normative and the structural elements of any social system. They have also emphasised that the generation of new resources, leading to potentially new levels of structural differentiation, may be an important source of change and that it is the development of new value system that may create the major control systems through which such changes become institutionalized.

In the central thesis of 'symbolic-structural approach' of Claud Levi Strauss (quoted by Eisenstadt : 1978), concern has been the binary oppositions posed by the innate rules of the human mind. According to this approach, the symbolic transformation of such contradictions as those between culture and nature account for the transformation of social orders.

Don Martindale (1962) has pointed out that social change takes place as a result of exogenous and endogenous factors. An exogenous factor is one arising outside a social system whereas an endogenous determinant of social change is internal to the social system itself.

DIRECTIONS OF CHANGE

Why culture changes and why it assumes different forms ? Does a culture of a given population or area change as a whole, in togetherness, or also its various traits, elements and complexes change independently of one another ? These are some of questions which require conceptual clarity before venturing forth to analyse the process of social change in Bhotia society. In the process of change, the system often exhibit a form of change which is styled by the terms 'growth' and 'decline'. Growth and decline of a socio-cultural system may mean either its quantitative growth or decline, or qualitative growth or decline. It may mean these things in application to the whole system or to one of its components.

If a given culture, says Sorokin (1941), is a closely integrated empirical system, then it changes as a whole, in togetherness. He further says that, if a given culture is a system, but not closely integrated and consists, say, of several sub-systems, each with some margin or autonomy, then the leeway between the parts is greater; therefore only strong change in most important part (s) of it will be interlocked and will lead to the changes of the the culture as a whole, in its important compartments. If a given culture is the co-existence of several systems and co-existence of single congeries within outside the system, then such a culture must change differently in different parts, i.e.,

(a) all its important elements and components united into one system or suprasystem change together as parts of the whole;

(b) all its congeries—be they single element or systems that are congeries to one another—change independently from one another. The pattern, direction, rhythm,

> tempo of the change of the systems and of the congeries are profoundly different from one another.

If a society can be described as a system whose parts are mutually interdependent, then any change in its technology and general adjustments to the natural environment which presumably result in an effect on the social organisation should react on the system of the absolute logics; these in turn should react with each other and back again on the technology.

Firth (1951) suggests that any theoretical framework for analysis of social change must be concerned with what happens to social structure. He distinghishes between 'organisational change' and 'structural change'. The organisational change does not alter the basic relations between individuals and hence cannot be termed a change in the social structure. On the contrary structural change occurs when there is a modification in the basic relationship between members of a society. Firth's 'dynamic social theory' involves the idea of movement from one social condition to another. Such movement may be reversible or irreversible, gradual, rapid, it may occur in one major institution only or in several at the same time. It may be without noticeable disturbance of interpersonal relationship or it may be violent and disruptive. The analysis of social system by the dynamic social theory would demonstrate whether the social change is 'repetitive,' 'structural', 'gradual', or 'radical' (Worsley: cited by Firth, 1964). Firth further emphasises that, while discussing change, one should be well aware that 'continuity and change' are well integrated in the social system and one can study the changed situation only in comparison with the traditional.

ADAPTATION

The term 'adaptation' connotes to a varied shades of meaning in the anthropological literature. Therefore, it is quite imperative to deal with such meanings in a systematic manner and then finally sort out a framework of theory which corresponds to the present study.

Adaptation, Bennet (1976) says, "refers to the coping mechanisms that individuals display in obtaining their wants or adjusting their lives to the surrounding milieu to their lives and purposes". Rappaport (1971) says, "adaptation is a process by which organisms or groups or organisms, through responsive changes in their states, structures, components, maintain homeostasis in and among themselves in the fact of both short-term environmental fluctuations and long-term changes in the composition or structure of their environment". For Sahlins (1964), adaptation implies maximising the social chances. But maximisation is almost always a compromise, a vector in the internal structure of culture and the external pressure or environment". Richard Mazes (quoted by Bennet: 1976) in the IXth ICAES, proposes a scheme of the concept of adaptation that has the following points:

1. The term is all inclusive, which means that it can be used for physiochemical, biological and behaviourial or socio-cultural realms of phenomena.
2. It should be applied only to relations between the phenomena and the surrounding environment, and its criteria are 'necessity and relative merit'.
3. In the social—behaviourial level, adaptation has to be concerned with reference to the individuals, the groups, and the 'total cultural pattern'.
4. A detailed listing of adaptive domains'.
5. No adaptive domains exist for the 'socio-cultural hierarchy' that is social behaviour—and Mazes does not propose any.

Adaptation is also a key concept in two versions of system theory: the biological and behaviourial (e.g., Ashbey, 1952, and 1956) and the social (e.g., Berrien: 1968 or Buckley: 1967). In these references adaptation is usually defined as a process that permits survival, or survival in terms more gratifying to the organism tension reducing, changes as a result of adaptive responses.

Cohen (1971) says, "adaptation in man is the process by which he makes effective use for productive ends of the energy potential in his habitat". Every culture can be conceptualized as a strategy of adaptation, and each represents a unique social design. In man, adaptation is achieved by means of culture and its institutions whereas adaptation achieved by the population of mammals (e.g., growth of fur) is the result of genetic changes. The achievement of a viable relationship between the group and its environment always results from reciprocal modifications in the culture and in the habitat through changes in the group's energy systems and its organisations of social relations over a period of time.

Hardesty (1977) says, "adaptation is the process whereby beneficial organism/environment relationship are established." Alland (1970) says that there are really two kinds of adaptation—internal and external. In any integrated system, a change in one part requires compensation in other parts. No change is independent, all changes has ramifications throughout the system. Deriving idea from such a notion, Alland says, "external adaptation is the process of making beneficial adjustments to the environment, while internal adaptation is the process of beneficial compensation for those adjustments within the organism or other system. The study of adaptation, Alland suggests, must consider both kinds of adaptation.

Berry (1966) says, "the term adaptation is an ambiguous one. However, it refers to the changes in culture or behaviour which are associated with changes in an environmental setting". He classifies the varieties of changes (culture) under three categories—'adjustment', 'reaction' and 'withdrawal'. In the case of adjustment, behaviourial changes are in a direction which reduces the conflict (that is, increases the congruence) between environment and behaviour by bringing the behaviour into harmony with the environment. Berry says, this variety is one most often intended by the term adaptation and may be the most common form of adaptation. In the case of 'reaction' the behaviourial changes are in a direction which retaliates against the environment; these may lead to environmental changes which, in effect, increases the congruence between the two, but not by the way of culture or behaviourial adjustment. In the case of 'withdrawal' behaviour is in a direction which reduces the pressure from the environment; in a sense, it is a removal from the adaptive arena.

Sahlins (1964) has raised serious objections to the ecologcal framework. He has done this by readily admitting that what is there is there, but adding that if no system is demonstrated, we are reduced to the truism that populations that exist are in some sense adapted. This criticism has been countered (Harris, personal communication) by the suggestion that population exist below carrying capacity because adaptive systems must hedge against the poorest possible conditions. The population will adjust to the carrying capacity of the environment in its poorest yielding years.

Cohen (1968) says, "it is necessary to distinguish between 'adaptation' and 'adjustment' not only for purpose of clarity but also because even the adjustments within an adaptation alter the group's environment—however subtly—when it is concerned as total system of components. Adaptation and environment overlap to a considerable extent. But an evironment contains more than habitat and a group and its adaptation, it also contains the adjustments among the elements of adaptation. Adaptation and adjustment must be regarded as distinctive processes. The term adjustment and adaptation has also been used by O.H. Mowrey (quoted by Bennet : 1976) in a different but released sense : adaptation referring to responses or actions of individuals that have survival value for the individuals designed to reduce the particular tension or stimulation that triggered the behaviour. The term adaptation has often been reserved for social phenomena and functions, and adjustment being considered as purely psychological functions or process, as di Clyde Kluckhon (in his Navago Witchcraft, 1944, Kluckhon (1949) in one of his papers pointed out that adaptation and adjustment could not explain the whole of cultural behaviour since they were instrumentally oriented : that is, they ignored the creative and expressive elements in behaviour. If, however one approaches the problem of social exchange, or tension-reduction, then it can be held that all behaviour is adjustive, and all behaviour, including the expressive or creative behaviour, always will have some kind of adaptive or maladaptive functions or effect.

The process of adaptation takes place at three levels: behaviour psychology, and genetic/demographic (Baleson, 1963 ; Slobodokin 1968 ; Slobodokin and Rappaport, 1974). Each level includes several adaptive domains. Rapid adjustments to sudden changes in the environment take place at the behaviourial level. If the disturbance continues then psychological or second level mechanisms replace or support at the behaviourial level. Finally long term and permanent changes in the environment are combatted with mechanisms at the very heart of organism—genetic. At the time of environmental shock, all levels are activated simultaneously to reduce the impact of the stress. Behaviourial level is activated most rapidly, followed by the psychological level, and finally at the genetic level.

Although theories dealing with socio-cultural change and adaptation do not end here, in the present study, I have taken only those points or concepts which are relevant and tend to correspond to the process of change and adaptation in the Bhotia society. However, there are certain theories and concepts which directly correspond and refer to process of change and adaptation taking place in the Bhotia society. In the present research work, the analysis of the process of change and adaptation has been done in reference to the two theories : firstly, the externalistic theory of change as developed by Sorokin, and dynamic and causal forces of change, developed by Ryan who advocates to identify or determine the prime-mover or singular causal force for effecting change in the society under study. Secondly, for understanding the process of socio-cultural adaptation in the Bhotia society, I have based my discussion primarily on the line suggested by W.J. Berry who says that adaptation can be understood in three phases : 'adjustment', 'reaction', and 'withdrawal'.

Thus, against such a theoretical frame of reference, the present study is based.

2

Geographical, Historical & Ethnographic Settings of Bhotias

For administrative purposes, the Uttar Pradesh Government have divided the border regions of Central Himalayas into three districts namely, Pithoragarh, Chamoli, and Uttarkashi. These three districts, when referred to collectively, are known as Uttarakhand. Besides being the source of many rivers and abode of famous Hindu Shrines like Kedarnath, Badrinath, Baidyanath etc., Uttarakhand is peopled by a wide range of ethnic groups who provide it a vast spectrum of cultual types and heritage. Here, thc people of caste groups like Rajput, Brahman, Harijan or Shilpkar, and the Scheduled Tribes like Bhotia and Raji dwell in close proximity to each other. Though these people share a lot of common cultural traits, there are certain remarkable differences in their life-style which distinguish the caste groups from tribals and vice-versa. In Uttarakhand most caste groups are predominantly agriculturists. But the tribals e.g. Bhotia and Rajis, due to historical and environmental factors, have been leading a semi-nomadic and transhipmeant life which was, till recently,

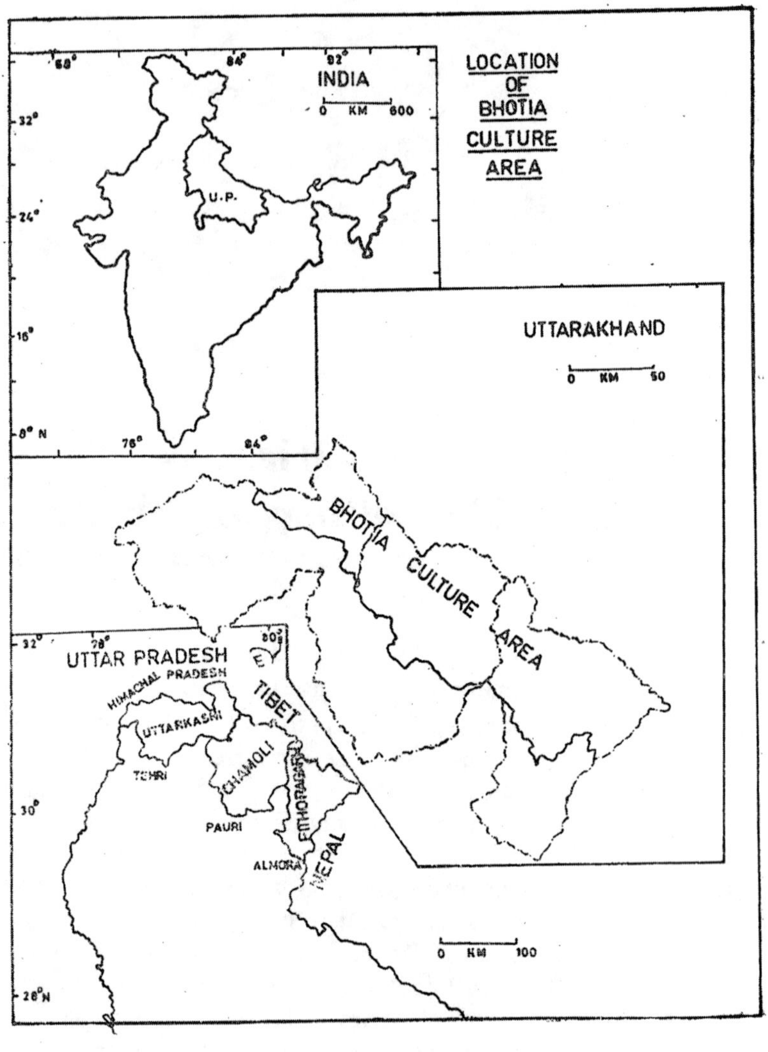
LOCATION
OF
BHOTIA
CULTURE
AREA
INDIA
0 KM 600
U.P.
UTTARAKHAND
0 KM 50
BHOTIA CULTURE AREA
UTTAR PRADESH
HIMACHAL PRADESH
UTTARKASHI
TEHRI
CHAMOLI
PAURI
PITHORAGARH
ALMORA
TIBET
NEPAL
0 KM 100

associated with the trans-Himalayan trade of the Bhotias and food gathering and hunting activities of the Rajis.

Besides the Bhotias and the Rajis of Uttarakhand. there are three other tribal communities in the state of Uttar Pradesh who are known as Tharu, Bhoksa, and Jaunsari. While the Bhotias and the Rajis are the mountain dwellers, the other tribals e.g., Tharu, Bhoksa and Jaunsari, are inhabited in the terai regions of the Nainital and Dehradun Districts of Uttar Pradesh. The numerical strength of these five tribal communities is 1, 98, 565 (Census-1971) and constitute 0.22 per cent of the total population of the states. Of this population, the Bhotias number 25377 and constitute 12.7 percent of the total scheduled tribe population in U.P. (Details of Bhotia population is given in Appendix-I).

The name Bhotia applies to the upper hill fribe of Uttarakhand inhabiting the giant mountains which separate India from Tibet. Bhotias, being the inhabitants of Indo-Tibetan border,a zone of ethnic admixture and cultural assimilation, show a close racial and cultural affinity to the Tibetans and most probably due to this similarity Bhotia region is addressed as Bod or Bhot, which is used as a synonym for Tibet, too. In their manner and customs they are more akin to Tibetans than to their Hindu neighbours. They have various local names. In district Uttarkashi they are known as Jaad Bhotias, in chamoli as Marcha and Tolcha, while the Bhotias of Pithoragarh are known as Joharis. and Shauka. The Shouka Bhotias are recognized by different names, namely, Byansi, Chaudansi, and Darmiya according to the name of the valley they inhabit. The different local names of the Bhotias viz. , Jaad, Tolcha, Marcha, Johari, and Shauka, are also the endogamous group of Bhotias who inhabit distinct mountain valleys which are separated from each other by snow clad mountain ranges, deep gorges, and declivities. Inter-communication between these valleys has been extremely difficult and dangerous. These Bhotia endogamous groups differ structurally and culturally from each other and the differences in the distribution of socio-cultural

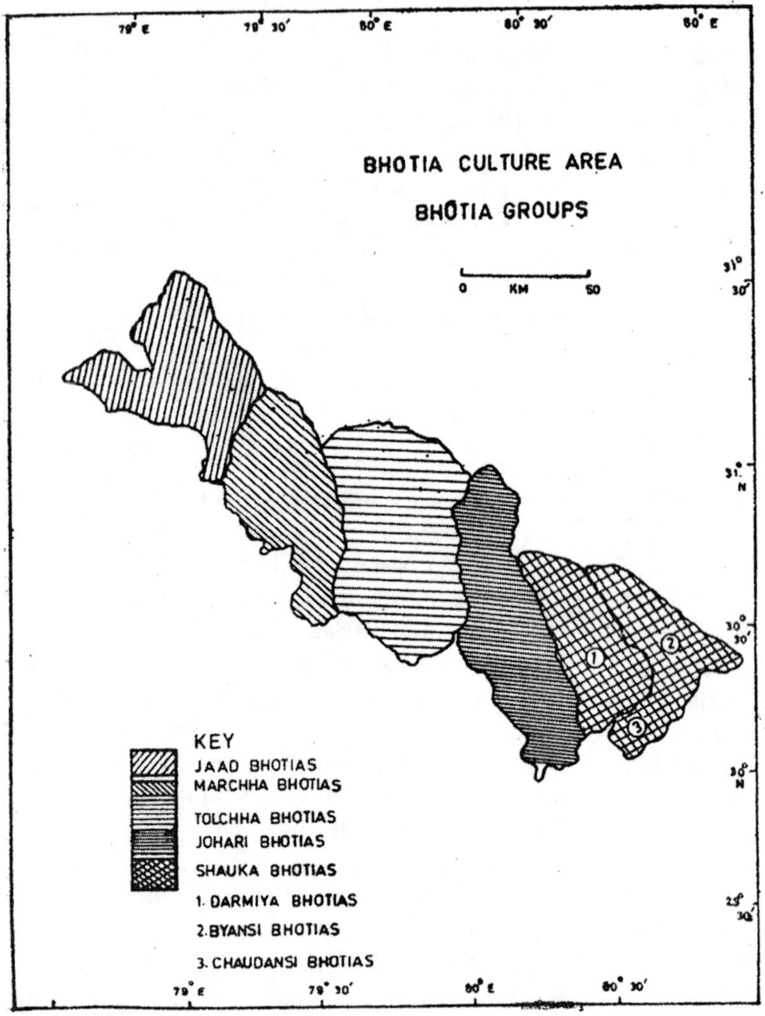
BHOTIA CULTURE AREA
BHOTIA GROUPS
0 KM 50
KEY
JAAD BHOTIAS
MARCHHA BHOTIAS
TOLCHHA BHOTIAS
JOHARI BHOTIAS
SHAUKA BHOTIAS
1. DARMIYA BHOTIAS
2. BYANSI BHOTIAS
3. CHAUDANSI BHOTIAS

components exist due to the differences in the environmental and historical factors. The five endogamous groups of the Bhotias are concentrated in seven valleys of Uttarakhand which are further divided, for administrative purposes, into smaller geographical and administrative units viz. Division, Districts, Tahsils. Thus, on the basis of the endogamous groups, valleys, administrative divisions, districts, and tahsils, of the Bhotia tribe can be represented in the following table (1).

TABLE– 1

Bhotia Groups of Uttarakhand

Sl. no.	Bhotia Group	Division	District(s)	Tahsil(s)	Valley(s)
1.	Johari	Kumaon	Almora Pithoragarh	Almora Munsiari	Johar
2.	Shauka	Kumaon	Pithoragarh	Dharchula	Darma Byans Chaudans
3.	Tolcha	Garhwal	Chamoli	Joshimath	Niti
4.	Marcha	Garhwal	Chamoli	Joshimath	Niti Mana
5.	Jaad	Garhwal	Uttarkashi	Bhatwari	Nilang Jadung

BHOTIA REGION AND ITS PHYSICAL BACKGROUND

It is rather difficult to clearly demonstrate or define the Bhotia region. Sir J. Strachey (quoted by Atkinson) has rightly remarked "the limit of Bhot (Bhotia region) in these districts cannot be very strictly defined, for the term is an ethnographical rather than a geographical expression, and signifies rather the tract inhabited by the Bhotias which, too, has varied from time to time, than a country of which any positive boundaries can be named". Talking about the boundary of the Bhot tract Atkinson (1882) said, "it will give a fairly correct idea of the general limits of the Bhotia tract if we consider it to be bounded by a line passing through or perhaps a little to the north of the great peaks of the Himalaya. In Kumaon one line of demarcation is somewhat clearly defined, but in Garhwal, to the west of Trisul, the line of perpetual snow recedes some twenty miles north, and the Bhotia boundary follows". Precisely it may be held that the region inhabited by the Bhotias lies in the extreme northern part of Uttarakhand, it stretches in a belt from east to west between 84° 30′ North to 84° 31′ 30″ North Latitudes and 78° East Longitudes. It encompasses an area of 5000 square miles of the total area of Uttarakhand division i.e. 9331 square miles. Administratively, it includes pargana Johar and three pattis of pargana Darma of District Pithoragarh, pargana Malla Painkhanda of District Chamoli and a small northern part of District Uttarkashi. On the north it is bordered by the lofty snowy ranges from Tibet. The river Kali on the east separates it from Nepal. On the south the greater part of pargana and pattis of the three districts of Uttarakhand i.e., Pithoragarh, Chamoli and, Uttarkashi. A small portion of the region lies in district Uttarkashi bounded by the river Gangotri in the South and by one of its tributaries from the West.

The entire region falls under the greater Himalayan System of the Central Himalayas. The physical landscape of the region is characterized by its lofty snow-clad peaks, glaciers, irregular line of mountain ranges with sporadic distribution of vegetation, deep & narrow river valleys, and precipitious streams. The only parts of the Bhotia region which are inhabitable and capable of cultivation are the narrow valleys lying between the great peaks which run down to the south from the water-parting of the chain, and in which flow the tributaries of the Ganges on the West and the Kali on the East. The climate of the region is strongly governed by the direction and latitude of the mountain ranges and nature of valleys, which produce extreme local climatic variations within short distances. The main distinguishing characteristic of the climate of this region which differentiates it from other parts of Kumaon and Uttarakhand is its lone and severe cold winters and moderately cool and short summers. According to Pant (1935), "the Bhotia culture area, situated in temperate latitudes, within the Himalayan system and far from the marine influences, in general represents Koppen's and Flahault's climate types i.e. Hekistothermal and Microthermal, with certain marked anomalies". In the Bhotia region, the largest monsoon rainfall takes place on the ridges that lie on the south of the snowy peaks or in the valleys exposed to the direction of the monsoon and as we move northward, behind the snowy ranges, it is almost negligible. With the increase in the altitude, the temperature rapidly decreases, the approximate average being a fall of 1° F for every 300 feet. This decrease in temperature is more rapid in summer than in winters. Stmilarly, the barometric pressure also diminishes with increase in altitude. At a height of 5,000 feet, the pressure is about 25 inches, at 10,500 feet it is about 16 inches. The velocity of wind is very high in the high altitudes and there are blizzards sometimes of the velocity of about 150 Km. per hour. In the valleys, which are protected by high ridges, such a phenomenon is most uncommon.

ALTITUDINAL RANGES

The Bhotia region can be divided into the following five altitudinal ranges :

(1) *Areas above 600 meters*

The whole of this range, with the exception of the deeper river valleys, lies above the limits of perpetual snow. It is characterized by a highly rugged mountainous topography, and an entire absence of vegetation.

(2) *Area between 3900 and 6000 meters*

The main part of this range lies between the great snowy ranges and the Tibetan watershed in the north while it also occupies narrow tracts the south-eastern slopes of the main ranges. This zone is entirely beyond the limits of human habitation and natural vegetation. It represents the glacial region of the Bhotia culture area.

(3) *Area between 2700 and 3900 meters*

This zone roughly accounts for the area falling in the upper reaches of the river Jaad Ganga, Vishnu Ganga, Gori Ganga, and Kutiyangti. In this area we find the summer villages of Bhotia, because this range or area remains covered with snow for more than half of the year. Due to the climatic conditions this area is suitable only for single crop cultivation. But this area has got special significance for the Bhotias it provides the alpine pasturage or 'bugyal' to their cattle.

(4) *Area between 1500 and 2700 meters*

This zone roghly corresponds with the lower valleys of the river Darma, Kutiyangti, Gori, Vishnuganga, and Dhauli. It is the most important region of the Bhotia culture area from both economic and habitational point of view. The winter dwellings of the Bhotias are found in these valleys because it relatively provides greater opportunities for cultivation and shelter during the severe winter.

(5) *Area below 1500 meters*

This range is mostly characterized of the precipitious banks of the rivers, and altitude is conspicuously absent while in the east it roughly corresponds with the river valleys of Gori, Dhauli and Kali.

JOHAR VALLEY : THE STUDY AREA

JOHAR is a large pargana in the Munsiari tahsil of Pithoragarh District with a length of about 65 miles and a breadth of 24 miles. On the south it is bounded by parganas Sina and Askot, on the east by Tibet and pargana Darma ; on the west the eastern Ramganga flows between it

MAP OF MUNSIARI TEHSIL
DIST. PITHORAGARH

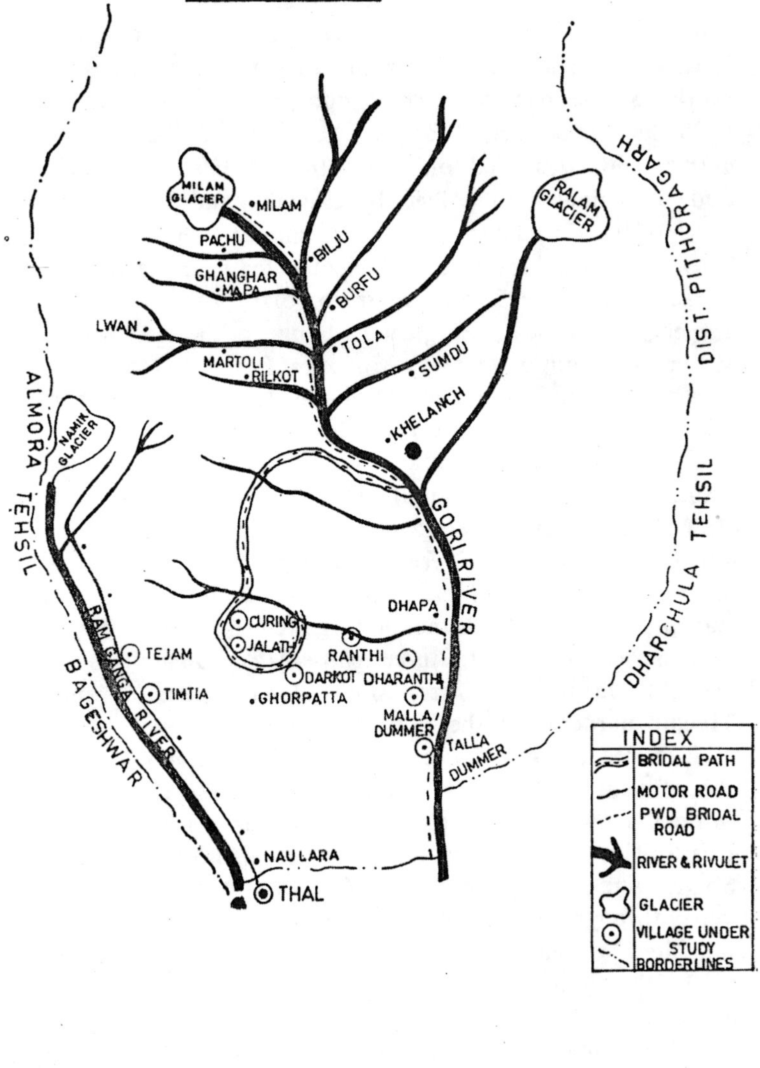

and Danpur and the boundary is continued by the chain of snowy peaks extending northwards from Nandakot, beyond this barrier lies the Painkhanda pargana of Garhwal. The northern boundary is Tibet. The range traversed by the Untadhura pass extends from east to west across the north of the pargana. The region to the north of the pass is for the greater part of the year ice-bound and desolate and until recently was used only by the Bhotias while making trade excursions into Tibet by Balchha and Shelsel passes. South of the Untadhura pass rises the eastern branch of the Gori, whose headwaters are principally fed from glaciers lying at each side of the Bhotia road to that pass. The western branch rises in the great glacier lying to the north-west of Milam, and both unite below Milam to from the Gori. Glacier streams descend from Nanda Devi and the Laspa torrent from Nandakot and join the Gori on the right bank. On the left bank, the most considerable feeder is the Ralam river, which rushing between the Hansaling (18,100 feet) and Dhansi (18,200 feet) peaks joins it below Bagdwar. The main road into Johar branches off from the Pindari glacier route at Kharbagar above Kaphkot, and proceeds by Ramari on the Ramganga across the Kamundi range to Suring and Lilam.

Johar is divided into three pattis-*Malla Johar, Goriphat,* and *Talla Johar.* Of these, Malla Johar extends from the Tibetan border down the Gori valley as far as its junction with the Ralam river. The fifteen villages comprised within the boundaries of the Malla Johar Patti lie with one exception in the narrow gorge occupied by the upper course of the Gori river. The northern most village of all is Milam and further South again is Laspa and east of Laspa is Ralam in a side valley through which flows the Ralam river. Malla Johar is inhabited by Bhotias and their Dom or Shilpkar servants. Their villages are for the greater part above the limit of cultivation and even in some cases of trees.

All the village of Malla Johar are situated at elevations exceeding 10,000 feet to the north of the great snowy peaks and between them and the line of water parting which forms the boundary towards Tibet. During the winter the whole of the valley is blocked with snow and the villages are abandoned. The Bhotias move down to their winter houses or encampments in patti Goriphat where the fine slope of the Kalamuni range as far as the Gori river is occupied by the villagers of Suring, Gorpatta, Daranthi, Dummer etc. which together from the tract known as *Munsiari*, the tahsil headquarter.

Talla Johar and Goriphat occupy the tract to the South of Malla Johar. They are separated by the water parting ridge between the basins of the eastern Ramganga and Gori. Goriphat, as its name suggests, comprises the valley of the Gori to the east, and '*Talla Des*' lies between the central ridge and the Ramganga. The inhabitants of this tract are in the main ordinary Khasiyas but a few non-trading Jethora Bhotias hold a fair number of villages. The tract is fertile though somewhat wilder and more thickly wooded than the central pattis of the district. The main Kharif crop is *mandua*, and a little rice is also grown in the warmer villages.

STUDIES ON BHOTIAS

Bhotias are a fascinating group of tribes with interesting cultural characteristics which show systematic variation from one valley to another. The Bhotia tribe so far has not been subjected to what may be called a thorough and systematic anthropological and sociological study. Not that they have not been studied or described. But whatever work has been done is either unsystematic, scattered, or scanty and of uneven quality. Moreover, while tribal people of a single valley or contiguous valleys has been studied together, there are very few studies where Bhotias of all the seven valleys have been sought to be brought under the same rubric. Living for most part of their existence in the Himalayan fastness and the arid tableland of western Tibet, Bhotias have developed their own distinctive cultures in the broadest sense of the term. They have their own style of dress, rituals, customs, popular beliefs, farming and business methods, and language. But due to the relative inaccessibility of their natural habitat, the Bhotias have tended to be somewhat isolated. However, pilgrims, travellers, explorers, administrative officers, and later social scientists came in touch with them and have left a body of scattered and unsystematic literature on the Bhotias in the shape of sporadic papers and sketchy description in some handbooks, gazetteers, settlement reports, and in a few preliminary anthropological essays and field reports.

The earlier writings dealing with the Bhotias belong to the late nineteenth century. They are very interesting, but are virtually unclassifiable into one or another recognized disciplines like sociology, ethnology, or geography. Their basic orientation is global, and comprehensive with sharp attention to details, but devoid of finer analysis in general. The earlier gazetteers, census tracts, and administrative reports of land settlement etc. belong to this genre. The accounts of travellers, geographers, pilgrims and administrators give some very fascinating accounts of these people. Accounts of Traill (1832) and Atkinson (1882, 1884, 1886) are representative of this class of writings. The work of Sherring (1906, 1966) belonging to a somewhat later period, has rightly become a classic containing very good observations about the Bhotia he came in contact during his travels in *Chaudans*, *Byans*, and *Johar* valleys. He has included description of mountain passes in the region between *Unta Dhura* on the West to Hoti and Niti on the West such as '*Sanchomala* , *Balch Dhura*, and *Lapthal*, which find rare mention in existing literature.

Books written by explorer-geographers like Sven Hedin (1910, 1913) and Swami Pranavanand (1953) are scientific treaties in which Bhotias as tribal people have been treated with meticulous care. Writing of Rahul Sankrityana with their heavy slant towards history and archaeology are somewhat of uneven quality : educated Bhotias challange the authenticity of some of the accounts of Sankrityana, on grounds of containing some glaring errors.

From about the second decade of the present century writings on the Bhotias started becoming more sharp, focussed, analytical and discipline oriented, rather than loose, global and unselective. Authors like Pate Ram, Panna Lal and S.D. Pant (1935) have dealt with selected aspects of Bhotia life and culture in considerable detail and precision. This tradition has grown, though not very vigorously, and now we have the scholarly contributions from authors like R.P Srivastva (1953, 1958), S.C. Tiwari (1954, 1955), H.C. Upreti (1965, 1968), H.P. Upreti (1967, 1968) R.P. Upreti and few others who have enriched the scientific literature on Bhotias, so that we can say that what may be called anthropology, geography, economics, and psychology of the Bhotia people are slowly but surely taking shape.

Another major category of literature in which Bhotias figure sometimes quite prominently is the extensive accounts of travels by travellers and pilgrims to sacred and holy places which lie within or beyond Bhotia land. This literature is quite extensive, and most of it is in native languages like Hindi, Bengali, etc. The world famous Badrinath shrine is on Alaknanda, only 3.1/2 Km. downstream from Mana, the large and ancient village of Marcha Bhotias. The most popular route to the holiest of holies, Mount Kailash and lake Mansarover involved crossing the Lipulekh pass beyond Chaudens and Byans valleys. The pilgrims and travellers came in intimate contact with the Bhotias, some of the pilgrims and travellers have left fascinating accounts of the Bhotias in their travelogues. But, some of these writers have failed to distinguish between Bhotias and Garhwalis, Kumaonis and Dotials of lower altitudes. Some have been confused Bhotias with Tibetans.

The main reasons for this slow rate of growth of scientific studies on Bhotias are two :

(a) The Bhotias reside in places which are reached only with considerable difficulty, and

(b) Security clearance has to be obtained from the Home Department and the Defence Department before one is allowed to visit the border areas in Himalayas, where the Bhotias inhabit.

HISTORICAL SETTING

Although the Bhotias of Uttarakhand exhibit certain cultural similarities with the people of Bhutan, they do not actually belong to the same ethnic group. The Bhotias of Kumaon, however, should not be confused with people of Bhutan who are really of Tibetan stock (Pangtey—1949). Diverse views have been put forward regarding the origin of the Bhotias. Though the Bhotias believe that they are originally Hindus and claim Rajput origin but their faith cannot be established on good grounds. Many of them believe that they are the direct descendants of God Ramchandra of Oudh. The inhabitants of this place prefer to maintain their relations only with the Kshatriya people. Whatever might be their origin it is more than sure that their original homes were not in the Hills of Kumaon (Banerjee, 1964). It is very difficult to distinguish between myth and fact. Though it is true that Tibetan and Chinese historians do speak of Rajput colonies in Tibet in the earliest time, but whether Hindus or not, there is no doubt that they are Mongolians (C.A. Sherring, 1906). According to another view, the Bhotias belong to the Tibetan stock since they show close similarity with the Tartar characteristics of the Tibetans in their physical appearance. Webber (1902) remarks that they belong to one of the "branches of the Huns which was driven south by other Tartar races, no doubt, was stopped by the Himalayas and preferring these wilds and a nomadic life, has remained in the inhospitable country even since". Spate (1964) also shares the same view and observes that, "Bhotia, Bhot, Bhoti, Bhutia, etc. all Tibetan and are applied to different tribes from the Punjab to Bhutan".

A similar view is also expressed by Sherring as he also traces their origin from the Tibetan stock: "The Bhotias are of Tibetan origin, though they themselves have still current among them the belief that they were originally Hindus." He further says, "That the Bhotias left Tibet before writing was introduced into that country about 650 A.D.', As against this view, Walton (1921) holds the opinion that, "The Bhotias are not by any means identical with the present Tibetans, though their features are of an undoubtedly Tartar caste. Pandit Rahul Sankrityan (1953) totally disagrees with the above mentioned views. He asserts that while some anthropologists confuse them with Tibetans of Mongoloid origin on the basis of certain similarities in language, customs and physical appearance, they are originally Hindu and most probably of Rajput origin. Hence both the views give diametrically opposed opinions on the origin of the Bhotias.

It is very difficult to trace out correctly who these people are, when and where they came from, and who contributed to the present Bhotia population. Majumdar (1962) observed that, "no anthropological study of this tribe has been undertaken so far and our information about the race elements in the population of the Himalayan region is extremely meagre". However, we can throw some light on the racial elements and cultural affinity of the Bhotias by making a probe into their cultural history, history of the names places of and linguistic evidence, etc.

In the absence of documentary proof, lack of archaeological evidences and a complete absence of direct evidences of ethnic stock who occupied this region in prehistoric times, it is very difficult to determine correctly the earliest entrance of man in this (Bhotia) region. Some details of the tribal population inhabiting the hilly tracts of Kumaon region are available from the Vedic literature as well as the two great epics of early Indian literature, the Ramayana and the Mahabharata.

According to the ethnographic records from the Vedas, it is clear that three classes of people dwelt in the upper part of India—the aboriginal tribes, people akin to Aryans but who had independent religious system and, a branch of Aryans. But it is somewhat difficult to find out correctly the direct and unbroken connection between the various earlier immigrants, who occupied this area and the present Bhotia population. In fact, "What little historical records exist show us great waves of invasion and conquest over all upper India from the earliest times and bitter dynastic and religious struggles. The many different tribes who joined in these wars have not been superimposed without disturbance, one on the other like deposits of inorganic matter, so as to enable us like the geologist at once to declare the order of their coming from their ascertained position, but rather they are in the position of a range of mountains full of faults, inversions and folds" (Atkinson, 1884).

The ancient records give various names to the different non-Aryan aborigines such as *Kinnars*, *Gandharva*, *Asuras*, *Yammunas*, etc. inhabiting the Himalayan region during the prehistoric period. The principal ancient aboriginal tribes, which formed the bulk of population at that time, were *Kirats*, *Tanganas*, and the Asuras. According to the Puranas, the tribes inhabiting this region were mostly *Kols* and the Kiratas (Kedarkhand, chapter 206, verses 2 and 3).

The Kiratas were of mongoloid origin, and due to their primitive way of living, they were recognised as a barbarous people (Sorensen, 1963). They were perhaps the first to arrive in this region. It is very likely that these people, the Tibeto-Burman speaking Mongoloids with yellow complexion, came to be known among the Vedic Aryans as the Kiratas. Their presence is attested through evidence as in the Yajur Veda and the Atharva Veda by about 1000 B.C. The Kiratas are also mentioned in other early Sanskrit work like the Mahabharata and Manu Samhita.

Some historians believe that the Kirata entered India through the north-eastern passes, followed by other tribes of Mongoloid stock. Karve (1962) says, "the same corridor of migration admitted mongoloid people who spread through Assam into Burma and represent the Tibeto-Burman stock. The same stock has penetrated into India along the whole Tibeto-Indian frontier including the central Himalayas". It is also held by Sankritayan (1953) that they (Kiratas) spread slowly in the Lesser Himalayan region, and later occupied almost the entire Himalayan region.

Although, due to scanty details and fragmentary archaeological evidences, the economic organisation of these people cannot be correctly estimated, it is, however, certain that a pastoral economy existed among the Tanganas, as was the case of their Kins i.e., the Kiratas. In Mahabharata, occasional references to the Tanganas reveal that they carried out trade in gold. There is also some remarks about a northern tribal, which occasionally brought presents of gold to '*Yudhisthira*' and had been present at the Rajasuya (Sorensen, 1963). They were perhaps the chief carriers of trade in gold dust with Tibet. The Tanganas also brought 'Lecha' salt from Tibet to India, a practise which was most widespread among the Bhotias until recently. In the absence of a common language they resorted to a peculiar method and covered the heaps of their merchandise with both hands and did not lift their hands until they got the desired cost. It appears from the Mahabharata that the Tanganas brought gold dust, beautiful '*Chaunwar*' (the tail of the mountain cow used in hand-fan), Himalayan Khudramadhue (honey), precious stones for garlands and sacred water from Uttar Kurudesh and 'Mahavala', drug from Kailash in north in the Rajasuya-yagna of Yudishishtra. Yodhyan has also described their food habits and other economic practices and it is mentioned that they dealt in wool, drank wine, sold sheep and goats and carried trade in ornaments (Dabral, 1965).

Strikingly, such trade practices reveal close resemblances to those carried on by the Bhotias during their trade transactions with Tibet and parts of Northern India. Though such methods progressively vanished with cultural advancement, the earliest form of trade by the Bhotias was perhaps carried on in a similar fashion often referred to as 'Gamgiya'.

Thus relying upon the description given in the Puranic literature and considering the similarity of economic and social practices among the ancient Tanganas and the present Bhotias, it may not be incorrect to trace their origin from the Kiratas (Tanganas). But owing to their admixture with later racial groups who occupied this region during different times of its history, they have not retained the inherent characteristics of their ancestors.

About the first quarter of the seventh century, during the period of the Tibetan Emperor Strong-tran Campo, the entire northern part of the Himalayas from Assam to Gilgit in Kashmir was under his dominion (Sankrityan: 1953) and the entire region was termed as '*Bhotanta*': "The Bhotanta country is said to be here extended from Kashmir and lay to the west of Kamrupa and to the south of the Manasesa, Bhotanta is evidently Bhotan and Manasesa refers to the God Siva at the Manas lake (Manasarovar) in the Himalayan (Sircar: 1960).

The study of Bhotia dialect gives valuable evidences in reconstructing their relation with the ancient kiratas (Tanganas) and the Tibetans. According to Rahul Sankrityan (1953) in the dialect of the Bhotias of the Byans Valley, the word-Mina (Ma), Chumai (Beti), Ti (Panit), Maidu (Aag), Cham (chalna), etc. are remnants of the dialect of Kiratas, from which their original ancestors appear to be the Kiratas. The dominance of the Tibetan influence is clearly evidenced in the nomenclature of several Bhotia villages. In the entire region, there are several places which indicate a Tibetan origin. Place names carefully used provide much valuable insight. Some of the place names, such as Tingding, Bungnal, So Sungnal, Dung Tung, Sosa, Rung Kang, Dung, Garbiang, etc. have close resemblances to those in Tibet.

All these evidences give us sufficient proof that the Bhotias are essentially of Mongoloid origin and the present population is an intermediate group, perhaps more closely related to the Tibeto-Mongoloid race than to any other.

FISCAL HISTORY OF BHOT

The name BHOT is applied to refer only to the Himalayan ranges, which once formed a part of the adjacent Tibet province of Bhot. Since the annexation of that tract to the divisions of Kumaon and Garhwal of Uttar Pradesh, a portion of the neighbouring pargana has been incorporated with the several villages known as *Bhot Mahals*. These villages have mostly remained in the occupation of the Hindu properties.

Bhot was for a long time ruled by the semi-independent Rajwars of Askot on behalf of the Chand Rajas, but the Bhotias have always admitted to the claims of Tibet to suzerainty "as anomalous state of subjection which their paramount interests in continuing to be the medium of commercial intercourse between Hindustan and Tibet will tend to perpetuate (Trail, 1825). The Bhotias paid revenue to the Tibet Government in the form of taxes which consisted of sinhthal (land revenue), yathal (tax on sunshine), Kyumthal (tax on the profits of trade). But the revenue exacted by their (Bhotias) Hindu conquerors have, according to Trail (1825), even been more costly and extensive. On their final subjugation the Bhot mahals were subjected to a tribute in gold dust. The assets which came under taxation were profits of trade, tandkar or loom tax, produce of agriculture, produce of jungles, musks, hàwks, and wild bees' nest. The tax was levied alternately on land and on property.

In 1815 the British conquerred the district. Mr. Gardener, the 1st Commissioner, made the 1st settlement report of Kumaon. This was based on the pattern of the Gorkhas revenue assessment system with the difference that the tax was not realised in the Gorkha currency, but on Farukhabadi rupees which resulted in a reduction of the nominal assessment by 25 per cent. Mr. Trail made the second settlement in 1817 and levied taxes on the trade, musk, bees wax, and hawks which resulted in the reduction of revenue to a total of Rs. 4,130 on Johar, Darma, Byans, and Chaudans. The settlement in 1840-41 was made by Mr. Batten, who considered that Mr. Trail had made an excessive sacrifice of revenue by taxing only the produce of the fields and the forest. He imposed tax on the Bhotia villages which is calculated not only from on their land, which is of little value, but on their profits. Batten (1851) remarked, "it is quite fair that they (Bhotias) should pay, because they occupy an immense tract of country to the exclusion of all others. For six months they graze their sheep and cattle all over the country. They have the benefits of the roads and bridges made at a great expense, and with those advantages they make great profits, while they pay almost nil to the Tibet Government." Mr. Beckett in 1872 and Mr. Goudge in 1902 followed the principles of Mr. Batten and taxed the Bhotias on their general prosperity derived from whatever source—trade or agriculture—and assessed them at Rs. 7,883 and Rs. 10,255 respectively. Subsequent to the Goudge's settlement and until the attainment of Independence in India, the Bhot Mahals were governed in the lines directed by Goudge. For the internal management of those Bhot mahals the only public officer retained in them is the Patwari, who receives from the village Burhas (headman) the amount of their revenue or jumma for remitting the same to the 'sadar' treasury.

ETHNOGRAPHIC SETTING

Appearance

Bhotias are predominantly mongoloid in racial characteristics. They are of medium stature having yellow brown complexion with ruddy cheeks and dark brown eyes. They have black cymotrichous hair with scanty beards and moustaches, while their eye slits are oblique and epicanthic fold is commonly observed among them.

There is a wide variation in the distribution of these characteristics amongst the different Bhotia groups. The mongoloid characteristics are much more pronounced in Jaad and Shauka Bhotias than the Joharis, Marcha, and Tolcha Bhotias. Among the latter three groups, the Marcha Bhotias show a more pronounced mongoloid characteristics. Tolchas are having the least pronouncement of mongoloid characteristics and they look very much like the ordinary Garhwali people. The variations in the appearance of the mongoloid characteristics among the Bhotia groups are indicative of the degree of contacts and consequent hybridization of these Bhotia groups with the neighbouring Tibetans who are typical mongoloid people.

DIALECT

Linguistically all Bhotias of Uttarakhand belong to the Tibetan branch of the Himalayan group of the Tibeto-Burman family. All Bhotia groups are multi-lingual. They can speak Tibetan, Kumaoni and Garhwali dialects, besides of course, Hindi. But this multi-lingual quality is not found among the Bhotia women.

Each Bhotia group has a dialect of its own and quite often they cannot understand each other's dialect. The Johari Bhotias have decome so much Hinduised that they have forgotten their own dialect and employ the ordinary hill dialect. Sanwal (1977) has identified three cultural linguistic zones viz, (i) Bhotia, (ii) Kumaoni and (iii) Garhwali, in the hill regions of Uttar Pradesh. Walton (1911) observed that, "some (Bhotias) have so far become Hinduised that they have forgotten their original dialect and now speak the ordinary hill dialect common to their Khasiya neighbours, yet there are five living dialects still in daily use." The chief sub-division of Bhotias, classified according to their language, are the Jethoras, who speak Rankas and live in Goriphat, Malla Danpur, and Johar: The Tolchas and Marchas of Niti and Mana valley who have forgotten the old dialect and employ the ordinary hill language of their southern neighbours: the Rawats or Joharis of Johar valley who no longer use their own language, the Chaudansis and the Darmiyas who live in the pattis from which they derive their name and who speak their own language.

DRESS AND PERSONAL ADORNMENT

The dress material of the Bhotias is greatly influenced with the environment. Due to the cold climate in the high hills where Bhotias inhabit, their clothes mainly comprise woollen material, quite often home made.

The male dress mostly consists of the coat, trousers, and a cap which is quite familiar also among the hill peoples. Traditionally, the most important outer garment of the Johari Bhotias consisted of a long frock-coat (Bakhu), woollen boots chequered colours (Bukcha), and a long white turban (tankha). With the escalation of cultural contacts, the attire of the male Johari Bhotias have considerably changed and now they dress more or less akin to the other civilized peoples.

The Bhotia females dress is quite different from the ordinary hill women. The Bhotia women wear a skirt, coat, shirt, and a waist coat. The Johari Bhotia women, besides these clothes, also wear a headgear which goes from one to one and a half yards down the back, and with which they cover their face. The Johari Bhotia women keep their waist portion covered without about 12 yards long cloth which is known as 'PAGRA'. These days some Bhotia women have begun wearing sari, petticoat, blouse, etc. The school going girls have almost abandoned their traditional costumes and wear the clothes of latest fashion.

FOOD AND DRINKS

The staple food of Bhotias consists of millets, potatoes, barley, rice, and wheat. They are very much fond of eating rice. The Johari Bhotias especially relish dehydrated meat, 'Sattu', and rice-beer. The Johari Bhotias donot eat beef whereas the other Bhotia groups were reported to be in habit of eating beef, but they too have now abandoned it. Sherring (1906) has observed, "the question of taking food with certain persons, and not with others, which is of absorbing importance to the ordinary Hindu, is treated in some respects very seriously, especially by the Johari Bhotias." In almost every household whether rich or poor, the day begins with simple tea. The practising of taking salted tea (Jya) with sathu prepared from parched wheat. At lunch time rice, lentil pulse, vegetables along with '*Chatni*' are generally taken. Among the Johari Bhotias it is a custom, also in other Hindu households, that men should eat first and then the women and children.

All Bhotias drink liquor, both fermented and distilled. The distilled liquor is made of rice and 'gur' while the fermented drink is brewed out of rice. The Johari Bhotias use spirit at the time of worshipping their ancestors and regional deities.

SOCIAL ORGANISATION

The Johari Bhotias are divided into 14 territorial clans and clan exogamy is strictly followed. The Johari Bhotias originally settled in 14 villages of Malla Johar. Each village was founded by a certain family which was later on regarded as founder of the village. The descendants of the founder family, with the passage of time, got labelled as the inhabitant (s) of a particular territory or village. To mark the name of the village with its inhabitants, a term "AAL" is suffixed in the name of the village or territory. Thus, among the Johari Bhotias, the name of their clans are based on the name of the villagers inhabited by them. From the following table (2) we can have an idea about the territorial clans of the Johari Bhotias.

TABLE—2

Territorial Clans of Johari Bhotias

Sl. no.	Village	Clan
1.	Milam	Milam-Aal
2.	Burfu	Burf-Aal
3.	Lowa	Low-Aal
4.	Paachhu	Paachp-Aal
5.	Mapa	Mapw-Aal
6.	Sumdu	Sumdy-Aal
7.	Laspa	Lasp-Aal
8.	Khelanch	Khinchiy-Aal
9.	Bilju	Biljuw-Aal
10.	Tola	Tolla
11.	Ganghar	Gangharia
12.	Ralam	Ralmw-Aal
13.	Mertoli	Mertolia
14.	Rilkot	Rilkotia

Each Bhotia clan is further sub-divided into several lineages and sub-lineages. The different clans of the Johari Bhotias enjoy various positions in the social hierachy in terms of heritage, economic prosperity, literacy, etc. The Johari Bhotias mostly prefer arranged marriages in which the groom's parents give certain amount of bride-price (BAKRAJ) to the bride's parent's which is a token for compensation to the loss of economic asset.

The Johari Bhotias, besides being divided into several clans, lineages, and sub-lineages, are divided into three distinct endogamous social classes which are known as *Bharet*, *Nitwal*, and *Kunkiya*. These three social classes are based on the consideration of ritual purity and pollution, and economic prosperity. The BHARET and the NITWAL Bhotias correspond to the ritually pure Bhotias whereas the KUNKIYA Bhotias are considered to be ritually impure, and hence, the Bharet and Nitwal Bhotias look down upon them and avoid intermarriage and inter-dining with them. The Nitwals are placed in the upper strata of the ritual purity by the Bharet and Kunkiya Bhotias. Nitwals are the immigrants from the Niti valley and due to their ritual purity and economic deprivation, they served as the cooks (Rasoyia) of the Bharet Bhotias. The Bharet Bhotias are incidentally both ritually pure and economically prosperous people whereas the Kunkiyas are economically downtrodden and ritually impure due to the historical factors. The Kunkiyas were employed by the rich Bharet Bhotias for doing odd jobs.

The economic system of the Bhotias is an aggregation of many elements such as a highly developed trade organization which got disrupted in 1962, subsistence agricultural activities, well developed handicrafts, pastoralism and regional sources of income. After the disruption of the Bhotias trade with Tibet, there has been a drastic change in the Bhotias' socio-economic set-up. The Johari Bhotias are having the most trying time in their economic history due to the stoppage of trade with Tibet.

The religious life of the Bhotias has been a peculiay blend of Hinduism, Animism, and Lamaistic Budhdhism. But with the increasing contacts of the Johari Bhotias with their neighbouring Kumaoni folk, who are predominantly Hindu, the Johari Bhotias have become highly Hinduised. Barring a few regional deities and spirits of the Bhotias, most of their gods and goddesses are akin to the Hindu people. The Johari Bhotias burn the dead bodies and offer worships to their ancestors.

In the field of political organization, the Johari Bhotias are maintaining law and social order through the institution of Panchyati Raj. In the bygone days, each Bhotia class was having its head known as 'Burrah'.The clan headman was entrusted to look after the village officers, arrange community level functions, and collect land revenues from the land holders. Though such traditional clan chieftainship is still in vogue, such headman or chiefs have no say in the village polity. They are only supposed to initiate and take part in the socio-religious ceremonies.

ETHNOGRAPHIC SETTING OF VILLAGES

Before examining the socio-economic conditions of the Johari Bhotias in the empirical situation, it is quite imperative to describe first the ethnographic setting of the Bhotia villages where socio-economic surveys were conducted. As described in the introduction chapter, the adaptive processes of the Johari Bhotia shall be studied in terms of the adjustment, reaction, and withdrawal ; the selection of the Bhotia villages was done by keeping in mind these points. For studying the adjustment and reaction processes, 8 villages were selected whereas the withdrawal scene has been studied from among the 8 places of Bhotia settlements. Thus, altogether 16 villages or Bhotia sites were studied which helped in collecting data from 224 Bhotia household. From among the 8 Bhotia villages, which corresponds to the Adjustment and Reaction Process of Adaptation, six villages viz., Malla Dummer, Talla Dummer, Darkot, Daranthi, Ranthi, Mapwalwada, are situated in Patti Malla Johar of tahsil Munsiari. All these villages lie on the Munsiari-Milam bridle path leading to Kailash and Mansarover. The river Gori Ganga flows beneath these village on an avarage distance of 5 k.m. The two other villages Tejam and Timtia are situated on the patti Talla Johar and lie at a distance of about 18 k.m. from Thal on the Thal Munsiari motor-road. The main concentration of population is in the centre of the village, and all the houses are clustered close to each other in one compact area. The main inhabitants of these villages are Bhotias who are surrounded with the few Thakur, Brahman and Harijan or Shilpkar families.

The withdrawal scene of the Bhotia families was studied from among those Bhotia settlements which have emerged out after the cessation of the trans-Himalayan trade of Bhotias. These settlements have grown up mostly in the urban centres like Thal, Bageshwar, Garur, Didihabt, Gwaldham, Pithoragarh, Almora and Haldwani. The distances of these urban centres from the tahsil headquarter Munsiari vary from 70 k.m. to 300 k.m. Of these urban centres, where Bhotias have immigrated after the cessation of their trade with Tibet, Thal is the nearest place whereas Haldwani is the farthest. From the following table (3) we can have idea about the Bhotia villagers and settlements selected for study.

TABLE 3

Sl. no.	Bhotia Village/ Settlement.	District.	No. of families studied.
1	2	3	4
1.	Talla Dummer	Pithoragarh	30
2.	Malla Dummer	-do-	19
3.	Darkot	-do-	40
4.	Daranthi	-do-	8
5.	Ranthi	-do-	6
6.	Mapwalwada	-do-	7

1	2	3	4
7.	Thal	Almora	20
8.	Bageshwar	-do-	9
9.	Garur	-do-	12
10.	Didihat	Pithoragarh	16
11.	Pithoragarh	-do-	2
12.	Almora	Almora	4
13.	Gwaldham	Chamoli	5
14.	Haldwani	Nainital	12
15.	Tejam	Pithoragarh	23
16.	Timtia	-do-	11
		Total :	224

While among the village of Malla and Talla Johar, the separate clans of the Johari Bhotias are inhabited, in the other Bhotia settlements, Johari Bhotias of different clans are inhabiting. Thus, such a distribution helps us in understanding the position of Bhotia people from the single clan, villages and multi-clan settlement. The 8 villages of Malla and Talla Johar viz. Talla Dummer, Malla Dummer, Darkot, Daranthi, Ranthi, Mapwalwada, Tejam and Timtia are occupied by the Johari Bhotia clans like *Biljuwal*, *Jangpangi*, *Pangti*, *Burfal*, *Mapwal*, *Rawat*, and *Dhamsattu* respectively.

3

Main and Subsidiary Elements of Bhotias' Economic Organisation

The economic organisation of the Bhotias' has undergone vast changes. In fact, the present economic set-up of Bhotias is the reorientated and modified form of the old economic order. The Bhotias' economy has been the aggregation of many elements such as a highly developed trade with Tibet, terraced cultivation, pastoralism, well developed handicrafts, etc. Of these elements, the Tibetan trade of the Bhotias' has been the principal element of Bhotias' economy because the other elements were largely dependant upon and associated with it. The Bhotias carried trade with Tibet for last several centuries. But, due to external factors i.e., the Sino-Indian border conflict of 1962, the Bhotias' trade, assiduously built up and passed from generation to generation, got disrupted. The cessation of the Bhotias' trade with Tibet has forced them to reorientate the course of their socio-economic life.

In the present chapter, which deals with the Bhotias' economic organisation, an attempt is made to describe how the Indo-Tibetan trade of the Bhotias formed the main pillar of the Bhotias' economy and also, how the other elements of the

Bhotia economy were dependant on the Indo-Tibetan trade of the Bhotias. The subsequent chapters shall discuss the impact of trade on the Bhotias' socio-cultural life, and the momentum of change which has been geared up by the collapse of the Bhotias' Indo-Tibetan trade.

In order to better understand the economic organisation of Bhotias, we can classify and then describe the main elements of Bhotias' economy under the following heads :

(*i*) **Trade**
(*ii*) **Agriculture**
(*iii*) **Pastoralism**
(*iv*) **Woollen Handicrafts**

Since the trade has been the main pillar of Bhotias' economy it would be desirable to lay special emphasis on its description which will give sufficient insight into the trading methods of Bhotias and its impact on the other elements of the economic system.

TRADE

The mountainous terrain of the Bhotia abode, half of which is snow-bound for almost half of the year and the other half not being very arable due to physical conditions, forced Bhotias to pursue a type of occupation other than agriculture. The border regions of Bhotia abode have a common boundary with the Western Tibet. The neighbouring province of Western Tibet and the sub-Himalayan District Pithoragarh, where Bhotias inhabit, are the regions of contrasted production. The former is bleak, barren, and inhospitable, and, till recently, depended entirely for its food supply and other necessities on the adjoining Indian district (formerly British-India) of Pithoragargh (formerly Almora). On the other hand, nature has provided it with some very valuable products such as high grade wool, a large number of drugs or medicinal herbs, valuable stones, yak-tails, furs, hides, skins, ponies, goat and sheep, borax and salt, etc. This contrast in production gave rise to a system of mutual exchange and trade. To facilitate trade transactions, the Pithoragarh got developed as a sort of forwarding or entrepot district. The inhabitants of this district acted as the middlemen because of their nomadic life-style and multilingual qualities. These middlemen were the Bhotias who held the monopoly of the whole trans-Himalayan trade from the Indian side. The trading system which developed between the Bhotias and the Tibetans was based on the mutual faith, barter, and a perpetual obligation on the traders of both the side. Over generations trade flourished in these regions and Bhotias specialised in dealing with their trade partners in Tibet. The Bhotias became an intermediary trading community between India and Tibet. The margin of profit earned by the Bhotias was very high and this made them as one of the most prosperous communities of the whole of Kumaon. Thus, it can be conceived that the dependance of the Bhotias of the Himalayas on trade, is neither of their own choosing nor is it the result of historic accident. A self contained peasant economy based on agriculture and animal husbandary could not be sustained by the natural resources of the Johar valley lying above 10,000 feet, and even below that level larger concentrations of populations could grow only where income from trade supplements the yield of subsistence farming.

The Bhotias developed trade relations not only with the Tibetans, but also with the local Kumaoni people, and the merchants of the North Indian market centres. Therefore, the trading system of the Bhotias will have to be discussed under two separate sub-headings :

1. Bhotias' Trade with the Tibetans and
2. Bhotias' Trade with the Local *Pahari* People and the Merchants.

1. Bhotias' Trade with the Tibetans

The trading system of the Bhotias with the Tibetans was mainly based on barter and mutual faith. It gave birth to many customs like *'sulchyu-milchyu'*, *'Gamgia'*, *'Sarji'* etc. and these customs, due to the uniqueness in its nature deserve separate mentions and discussions for developing an insight into the trading methods of the Bhotias. In discussing the Bhotias' trade with the Tibetans, it becomes imperative to mention about the trade routes and the trade taxes which the different Bhotia groups, including the Joharis, had to follow and pay. Thus, in order to describe the Bhotias, trade with the Tibetans, it is quite imperative to include the above points. For the sake of clarity, the entire trade complex of the Bhotias can be divided into the following sections :

(*a*) Trading Customs
(*b*) Trade Routes and Marts
(*c*) Trade Taxes
(*d*) Items of Export and Import
(*e*) Security Arrangements
(*f*) Trade Treaties

(*a*) *Trading Customs*

The Indo-Tibetan trade of Bhotias was based on a score of principles which, with the passage of time, became institutionalized and customary. Of the different trading customs, the following ones deserve mention and elaborate description.

(*i*) *Sulchyu-Milchyu*

The trade relation between the Bhotias and the Tibetans was based on mutual friendship and faith. But the friendship between the Tibetans was developed or initiated only after a formal ritual which is popularly known as 'Sulchyu-Milchyu'. The ritual of 'sulchyu-milchyu' used to mark the initiation of an everlasting partnership between two individuals i.e., the Bhotia and Tibetan, with regard to carrying out trade. The rituals connected with the 'sulchyu-milchyu' involved drinking of tea or wine in a special wooden bowl studded with silver, known as '*Furu*'. The 'Furu' was generally of such a size that it could be carried on in the pocket of the Bhotias' overcoat known as '*Bakhkhu*'. The Bhotia and the Tibetan, interested in initiating a trade partnership, used to drink tea or wine collectively in one and the same 'Furu' without caring for the touch-pollution. Actually this used to signify a greater sense of love and brotherhood between the two traders. The ritual to develop friendship between the two was simple act of consuming tea or wine followed by a feast. After the feast it was held that partnership between two individuals, interested in having trade relation with each other, was established. By drinking wine or tea collectively, it was also held that they have shared each other's religion. The trade partners were known as '*Mitra*' and each 'Mitra' was supposed to trade only with his fixed 'Mitra' developed by 'Sulchyu-Milchyu'. (A list of the Bhotia and Tibetan trade partners (Mitra) can be seen from the appendix no. 2).

(ii) Gamgia

In the beginning the trade was effected only between the fixed partners or 'mitras'. But, later on some traders tried to violate this rule of trade by trading with the other's 'mitras'. Such a breach of law gave rise to some problems in the successful and smooth running of the trade relations between the Bhotias and the Tibetans. Therefore, to overcome this difficulty, a written agreement of trade was introduced which was called as '*Gamgia*' (a true copy of the 'Gamgia' has been appended in the Appendix III). The 'Gamgia', which served as a written agreement for the Bhotias and the Tibetan traders was strictly adhered to by each trade partner. The trade partners were supposed to give a token or stamp of their symbolic representation in the trade markets. For this the trade partners used to split a piece of stone into two equal halves in which wool was wrapped along with a personal stamp or identity symbol of the each trader. The stamped halves of the split stone were known as '*Thanchiya*' and each 'thanchiya' was held by the two trade partners. Henceforth the Indian trader or his representative could carry the token and sell his goods in the Tibetan market only to his 'mitra' or the 'mitra's' representative who would fit his half of the stone to the Indian trader. It was held that the trade partners who violate the rule of 'gamgia' of trading only with the fixed partners, shall be required to pay gold equal to the weight of the 'thanchiya' to his 'Mitra'. In this trade system, however, there was provision to sell or buy the trade partnership to some other enthusiastic and interested trader. The written agreement of trade was supposed to be permanent and it was believed that so long sun continues to rise in the east ; there is water in the 'Mansarovar Lake', the agreements mentioned in the 'gamgia' shall remain valid.

(iii) Lakgirpa

Bhotias were supposed to trade only with their fixed partners. This sort of trade had its impact on stability of the market price between the two traders. To keep the rate of exchange of the goods secret between the two 'mitras', they had developed a symbolic method known as 'Lakgirpa'. The prices of the different goods and their rates of exchange were explained or indicated to the trade partners with the help of fingers and that also concealed within the overcoat or '*Bakhkhu*'. By holding the others hand inside the long capacious overcoat, "the unit of the exchange, (as observed by Charles : 1962), was stated like *Do di* i.e., *Do-tse*. When three fingers are gripped, three *Do-tse* are indicated. The seller continues *Tso di* i.e., *Tens these* and grips two fingers. Then *Pudi* i.e., *Sangs these* and four are gripped. The meaning of the whole is three Do-tse and twenty-four *Sangs*, for the *tens* refer to *Sangs*. A *Sang* was worth (in 1928) about one shilling and six pense, a *Do-tse* three pounds fifteen shillings". The buyer too makes his offer in the same manner. For six they took three fingers and turn them over, thus doubling the figure. For seven they used to hold five fingers and then two. Similarly, eight is four doubled, and nine is five plus four. This system is known as *'Lakgirpa'* because *'lak'* and *'girpa'* means hand and turning over respectively.

(*iv*) *Sarji*

The height and structure of the Himalayas act as an effective barrier to transport. The means of transport of the Bhotias viz. goat, mules, jibus, etc. were quite often subject to various diseases. For many a decade the Bhotias were oppressed by the *'gurkha'* and the local rulers. All this had a clearcut impact on the Bhotias' trade. Sometimes the entire trade season was spoilt due to the cattle's disease and 'gurkhas' invasion in the Bhotia region. Naturally, in turn this used to affect the Bhotias' trade partners in Tibet because they were dependant on the Bhotias for the supply of essential commodities. To avoid such a situation the *'Sarji'* system was evolved. In the 'Sarji' system, the Tibetans, on the eve of each year's trade season, started sending their representatives who were known as 'Sarji'. The 'sarji' used to enquire about the diseases of the cattle, and pack animals, threat of the enemy, and trade prospects. After enquiring about the affairs of the Bhotia region, the 'sarji' used to explain to Bhotias about the trade prospects of Tibet. When everything in each side was found alright, then the traders i.e., the Bhotias and the Tibetans, used to assemble at the marketing centres for effecting trade transactions. Thus, this system by which the enquiries about each other's region was made, came to be called as 'sarji'.

(*v*) *Trade Routes and Marts*

The Bhotias of different groups had to follow different routes and passes for entering into Tibet and use different trade marts or *'mandis'* for trading of the export and import items. The Johari Bhotias used to go to Tibet by crossing the *Untadhura Pass* (5387 metres). But in the bygone days the Johari Bhotias used to go to Tibet by crossing the *Ralam* pass. Since the route leading to Tibet through the Ralam pass was full of obstacles, ordeals, and risk of life, the Johari Bhotias abandoned it and explored the new route—the *Untadhura Pass.* Before reaching Tibet through the Untadhura pass, the Johari Bhotias had to make several halts in the en-route of their journey. The halts were made at fixed places. The first halt was made at *Jayanti* which was followed by the other halting places like *Dhura, Kukri-Bikri, Chircham, Topkubagar, Chilampani, Thajang, Chingu,* and *Darmayanti.* These halting places are situated at a distance rom 10 to 22 miles from each other. Before entering into Tibet, Bhotias had to pay certain trade taxes to the Tibetan trade agent.

Bhotias of different groups used to make the exchange, sale, and purchase of various commodities at the different trade marts or *mandis.* The trade marts usually frequented by the Johari Bhotias were *'Gyanima', 'Gartok', 'Darchin', 'Chakra',* and *'Shiva-chilam'.* Of these trade marts, the 'Gyanima' was the biggest trade mart. The 'Gartok' trade mart was the farthest and was used mainly for the trade in cattle.

(vi) Trade Taxes

The Bhotias going to Tibet for trade, had to pay a number of trade taxes levied on different items. But the amount and nature of taxes varied for different Bhotia groups. While the *'Shauka', 'Tolcha', 'Marcha,* and *'Jaad',* Bhotias paid taxes like the *'Chong-thal', 'Rong-thal', 'Ya-thal', 'Luk-thal', 'Tha-pka-thal', 'Du-thal', 'Chya-thal', 'Bha-thal', 'Chha-thal', 'ngan-thal',* etc., the Johari Bhotias had to pay only one tax known as *'la-thal'* or *'toche-rama'.* The *'La-thal',* was paid by the Johari Bhotias to the *'Jongpen's* (Tibetan trade agent) representative known as *'Satu'.* The 'la-thal' was given in the form of 90 *'bhelis'* of 'gur' or Rs. 45/- in cash. The 'la-thal' was collected by the headman (padhan) of Milam village of Johari Bhotias who, in consideration of his services, was allowed to have one riding pony, and free supplies of food and fodder during his sojourn in Tibet. The 'la-thal' collected by the 'pardhan' of the Johari Bhotias from the Bhotia traders was finally paid to the trade agent. In the beginning all Tibetans used to pay *'choo-thal'* or one tenth part of all goods brought from Tibet to Milam (Bhotia village). This was paid to Milmwal 'kamin' or headman. The Tibetans never raised any objection to this tax, but some forty years ago the British Government ordered that 'choo-thal' should not be levied, hence it was ultimately stopped. The popular term for the tax in the Tibetan dialect is *'thal'*. The Johari Bhotias, in comparison to the other Bhotia groups, had to pay only one tax i.e., the 'La-thal'. The Tibetan Government was committed to exempt the Johari Bhotias from the burden of taxes, barring 'la-thal', because, in the past, the Johari Bhotias had once saved the Tibetans from the robbers.

(*vii*) *Items of Export and Import*

In the initial stage of trade, Bhotias traded with the Tibetans mainly for the import of salt and borax. Bhotias used to supply these items to the *'pahari'* (hill) people of Kumaon and to the traders of the *'terai'* region. Borax was in great demand by the jewellers of the small towns and big cities. With the passage of time, the Bhotia's trade with the Tibetans grew both in quantity and quality. In the advanced stage of trade, the Bhotias established a good market for the Indian rice, barley, millet, wheat, clothes, etc. in the Tibetan market. From the table (4) we can see the detailed list of the items which were exported and imported by the Bhotias.

TABLE 4

Items of Export and Import

Items Exported to Tibet	*Items Imported From Tibet*
Sugarcandy, Gur, Confectionary, Almonds. Cloves, Chillies, Indigo, Pewter and Sal ammoniac, Coarse clothes, Pearls, Corals, Buttons, Chinaware, Grains, Hardware, Tobacco,	Borax, Salt, Golddust, Yak-tails, Ponies Sheep and Goat mules, wool, Pusham, Musk, Shawls, Blankets, Kuldar Rupees, Yak, Chinese dragon and other silk materials,

Betalnut, Satin jean, Velvet, Spices, Precious stones, and Jewellry.	Chouris, Zedory Nirbisi, and Saffron.

Bhotias used to obtain the items of export from the different marketing centres of India. They were having trade relations with the traders of Bombay, Delhi, Calcutta, Bhagalpur and other places. Besides these big marketing centres, the Johar Bhotias had relation on market terms with the 'Banias' (traders) of the 'terai' regions like Almora, Ramnagar, and Haldwani. Each Johari Bhotia trader was having his fixed 'Bania' of the terai regions, and the Bhotias used to call the 'Banias' as their '*Arathi*'.

The Bhotias had a very friendly relationship with the traders of both the sides i.e., Tibetan and the Indian traders. In India they used to buy the exportable goods from 'Banias' on credit or by making part payment with the assurance that the pending money or balance of payment shall be paid in the next year's transactions and this way a cyclic order of purchase and payment was made. Similarly, the Bhotias used to sell their goods with the Tibetans on credit or by receiving part payment with the understanding that the existing balance shall be cleared off in the following year's trade dealings. But this sort of practice had an unprecedented and devastating effect on the Bhotia traders which will be discussed in the subsequent chapter. From Table nos. 17 to 23 (see Appendix VI) we can have an idea about the amount of trade between Bhotia and the Tibetans, rates of exchanges, prices of different commodities, list of exports and imports in different years, and purchasings from the Indian market by the Bhotias, etc. These figures have been obtained from the George William Trail's book entitled, "Statistical Report on the Bhotia Mahals of Kumaon", 1878, p. 217-20. From these tables it becomes sufficiently clear that the Johari Bhotias were having a vigorous trading activities which involved a variety of goods and scores of money. The Johari Bhotias earned huge profits from this trade because of their trading skill, intelligence, and entrepreneurship. Atkinson (1882) has rightly remarked about the Johari Bhotias, "their intelligence is entirely the result of their own observation and experience. They seldom possess any education beyond the ability to read and write and to keep accounts of their trading operations". Commenting on the Johari Bhotia traders Atkinson says, "the Joharis are decidedly the most intelligent and most wealthy of all the Bhotias". An idea about the total exports and imports of various items like cloth, foodgrain, sugar, borax, salt, wool, etc, can also be had from the Table ons. 24-30 (see Appendix IV). These tables give a statistical account of the trade transactions of the Bhotias which were carried out by them between the years 1877 to 1883.

(viii) *Security Arrangements*

The Bhotias, while going to Tibet for trade, had to face a lot of problems. They were sometimes robbed by the robbers, mostly '*Khampas*', and their cattle were killed by the wild and ferocious animals. Sometimes the Khampa robbers used to drive away forcibly the cattle of the Bhotias. Therefore, to avoid such situations, Bhotias had made the habit of moving always in a group or with the horde of 50 to 100 persons. During their migratory operations and journey to Tibet, Bhotias were always accompanied by their dogs. The dogs of Bhotias, quite often known as Bhotia dog, are very ferocious and famous for their loyalty and obedience to their masters. In the night Bhotias used to kindle fire in a big heap of firewoods and sit around it. While some members of the horde used to sleep for sometimes, the others kept themselves wake up for keeping a vigilance on their cattle and other valuables. After 1947, when the Bhotias apprehended more dangers in their trade routes, then they approached the local officials and asked for the licences to keep pistol, gun, and rifles for the safety purposes which they were given. While in Tibet, the cattle of the Bhotia traders were looked after by their servants or graziers known as '*Anwal*'.

(*ix*) *Trade Treaties*

For the successful and smooth running of the trade, many trade treaties were signed between then British India, China, Nepal, and Tibet. The earliest treaty with regard to trade was signed in the year 1904 between British India, Tibet and China. In this treaty it was accepted py the Tibet Government that the trade passes viz. *Gyantse*, *Gartok*, and *Yortuk* leading to Tibet would always remain open for the Indians and no tax should be levied on them.

In 1908 another treaty was signed between Tibet and China in which the Indian traders going to Tibet for trade were given right on land to erect stalls. British Trade Agent was also appointed under this treaty who was assisted by the 'Jongpen'—trade agent of Tibet.

Simla conference held in the year 1914, in which the three countries participated Great Britain, Tibet and China, made the following treaties :—

Article (3)—British Government will not keep its force in Tibet and barring the officials appointed, and according to the treaty of 7th September, 1904, will not colonize the Tibet.

Article (7)—The rules of 1893 and 1903 with regard to Tibet trade are hereby declared null and void or invalid.

Article (11)—The present treaty will be put in force from the date of its signing.

In a treaty of 1951, it was declared that Tibet is a part of China, and consequent on the Chinese action in Tibet, India's relations with Tibet were placed on a new footing. On 29 April 1954 a "*Trade and Cultural Intercourse Agreement*" between India and China was signed with a view to facilitating pilgrimages and travels and to promote trade and cultural relations between "*The Tibet Region of China*" and India. In the Agreement, India unequivocally accepted Chinese sovereignty over Tibet. It was valid for 8 years and allowed the three Indian Trade agencies in Tibet to continue but established three Chinese agencies reciprocally at New Delhi, Calcutta and Kalimpong with equal status and privileges. Market, places of pilgrimage, routes for trade and pilgrimage were specified. The military escort of 200 jawans that the Government of India used to maintain in Tibet was withdrawn. The post and telegraph system which the Government of India had installed and maintained in Tibet was handed to the Government of China at a normal price. Finally, both sides gave a solemn undertaking that they would respect the territorial integrity and sovereignty of each other.

BHOTIAS' TRADE WITH NHE PAHARI (HILL) PEOPLE

The Johari Bhotias traded not only with the Tibetans and reaped huge profits, but also traded with the peoples of Kumaon. The hill peasants settled at low altitude villages are referred to as *Nangri Zimidars*. These people were largely dependent upon the Bhotia traders for the supply of *salt*, *wool*, *fur*, *skin*, *hides*, *cloth*, *meat*, etc. The Johari Bhotias used to barter these things with the *Nangri Zimidars* for the foodgrains, fruits, milk, curd, ghee, etc. which the pahari peasants or zimidars used to locally produce. A detailed account of the Bhotias trade with pahari people can be shown in the following discussion. These information and the following ones are based on the accounts furnished by Sri Ram Singh Pangtey (late) in his unpublished essay on the Johari Bhotias entitled as "*Johar Vansavali*". To quote Shri Pangtey.

"In the 18th century the Johari Bhotias traded with the pahari people or Nangri Zimidars in the form of money lending business. But they did not charge any interest on the advance or loan of rupees up to 25. Bhotias used to obtain the interest on their capital in the form of foodgrains. They used to charge 24 Rinias of rice as interest on 6 rupees per-year at the rate 4 Rinias rice for one rupee. This way the Bhotias started procuring foodgrains from the Nangri Zimidars. However, such trade dealings were done in the late 18th century. Besides the exchange of goods with money, the zimidars also exchanged the following items, with Bhotias imported goods.

12 'Tami' ghee,
few Nalis of rice, curd, vegetables, malta, orange,

With the Bhotias for,

1 'Belchi' wool
4 Nali Salt
1 Bheli gur, and dry meat, and fur.

In the late 19th century, Bhotias started effecting trade relations with the local peasants on purely barter system. They stopped lending money. But sometimes they did buy certain items from the zimidars on cash payment. The rate of exchange between the Nangri Zimidars and Johari Bhotias for different goods in the late 19th century were as follows.

The zimidars exchanged following goods
12 'Mana' ghee
1 'Tekha' curd
1 'Doka' banana, orange, and vegetables, *with the Bhotias for* :

1. 'Pankhi' (Woollen shawl)
1 'Belchi' wool
1 'Bheli' gur
1 'Bheli' tobacco
1 'Than' printed cloth, and
some dry meat."

But, with the introduction of the wheeled transport in the hills, and also due to the stoppage of the Bhotias' trade with Tibet, such a trade relation, which existed between the Bhotias and the Pahari peasants, was virtually stopped.

AGRICULTURE

The economy of the Bhotias is intimately related with their ecological and geographical conditions. How these factors determine the economic system of a society is clearly discernible in the case of Bhotia society. The rugged and terraced fields, inhospitable climate, scanty rainfall, and heavy snow fall in the Bhotia region provide no means of profitable agriculture. Pant (1935) says, "the agriculture of the region is thus very precious, and it is difficult to estimate the yield. It is sustained in these sterile tracks, under circumstances so discouraging, only on account of the Tibetan trade which is the mainstay of the people". Though Bhotias depended primarily on their trans-Himalayan trade. they did not give up agriculture. In fact, besides trade, agriculture has been one of the most important subsidiary occupations of the Bhotias.

Agriculture has been a subsidiary occupation of Bhotias, Walton (1928) says, "because their villages are for the greater part above the limit of cultivation and even in some cases trees. What little agriculture exists is of negligible value." The agriculture done by them is of primitive type and bears the imprint of environment, which is entirely different from the rest of Kumaon. The entire Bhotia culture area falls under the Himalayan system, which is highly mountainous and a greater part of the region lie above 15000 feet, above the sea leavel. In such relief conditions, it is not only uneconomical to practice agriculture but also an impossible task owing to the steep, rugged, and rocky slopes. Therefore, agricultural land is confined only along the gentle slopes, particularly where tributaries make more or less level plots before joining the main river. Due to the stony and uneven nature of land, cultivation is practised on small terraced fields. The structure of the terraced fields is directly related with the slope conditions. Though the area of Bhot region is one-third of the entire district, but only one-sixteenth is inhabited. The area under cultivations is smaller even than the area inhabited. Distribution of total land and cultivable land in some of the Johari Bhotia villages can be seen from the Table (5).

TABLE 5
Particulars of Land in Bhotia Region (Johar Valley)

Sl. No.	*Name of Village*	*Total Area in Acres*	*Forest*	*Irrigated*	*Unirrigated*	*Cultivable Waste*	*Area not available for cultivation.*
1.	Milam	346	164	—	136	36	10
2.	Pachu	492	312	—	80	98	2
3.	Ganghar	356	286	—	62	7	1
4.	Bilju	685	539	—	19	126	2
5.	Mapa	459	20	—	54	384	1
6.	Burfu	566	49	—	85	429	3
7.	Lwan	39	2	—	7	30	—
8.	Mertoli	303	83	—	68	148	4
9.	Toloa	282	45	—	67	168	2
10.	Sumdu	107	6	—	9	92	—
11.	Khelancu	604	24	—	44	535	1
12.	Ralam	794	72	—	36	685	1
13.	Rilkot	273	2	—	9	11	—
14.	Laspa	533	298	—	15	222	—
15.	Malla Dummer	90	13	T(1)F(1)	39	35	2
16.	Talla Dummer	210	36	T(3)F(3)	25	144	2
17.	Darkot	245	171	T(24)F(24	21	24	5
18.	Daranthi	258	16	T(22)F(22)	22	196	2
19.	Tejam	569	219	T(33)F(33)	95	217	5
20.	Timtiya	306	263	T(9)F(9)	8	24	2

T for tank and F for fountains

CROP AND CROP PRACTICES

Due to the severity of the cold climate and physical conditions, only one crop is grown a year in the Bhotia region. The main crops grown are *barley*, buck-wheat (phaphar and ugar, as locally known). rice, potato, and some vegetables like cabbage, and turpine. In the village where rabi crops can be raised in addition to the kharif crop, wheat and barley constitute the main crops, besides the summer crops of buck wheat, kauri, jhungora and potatoes. While wheat can thrive in much poor and drier solid, the cultivation of barley is usually restricted to well drained and rich soils.

In the Bhotia region, most of the agricultural operations are done by hand. The crop practices, as well as the implements used for it are very crude and display the scantiness of resources. Tilling operations are mainly done by the plough but owing to difficulties of terrain and the usually small size and irregularity of the fields, plough is not always practicable. The ploughs are clumsy and short, which are usually drawn by the jibu, a hybrid of the cow and the yak. Though now oxen are also used for this purpose, the cold climate of this region has led to a decline in their number. Quite often the poor Bhotias put their own family members to draw the plough.

LAND EXPLOITATIVE PATTERN OF BHOTIA TRADERS

Though the Johari Bhotias practiced agriculture as an important subsidiary occupation, they cannot be called as true agriculturist in the right sense of the term. This is so because Bhotias were themselves not involved in the agricultural operations. Their trading activities were itself so designed that they hardly got enough time for devoting in agricultural activities. During the summer i.e., from June to September, they used to remain in Tibet for trade transactions. After returning from Tibet they were required to dispose off the imported goods in the local markets, trade fairs, and other marketing centres. When all this was over, they used to go to the terai regions for purchasing the export items, etc. In doing all this about four months i.e., from November to March were spent. The remaining time was spent in the uphill and downhill migrations. Thus, it is evident that the traders Bhotias could not spare time for agricultural activities. But still, they did practise agriculture as a means of occupation and source of income. A simple question arises—how.

In fact Bhotias, until recently, never involved their labour in tilling their agricultural fields. For doing this they took the help of the pahari peasants who dwelt in the close proximity of their settlements of Goriphat and Talla Johar Pattis. These peasants were not only poor but also the marginal holders of landed property. The Bhotias, in contract to these people, enjoyed economic prosperity and commanded considerable size of land holdings. While the local peasants depended on Bhotias for procuring the commodities like salt, wool etc., the Bhotias depended on them for the exploitation and cultivation of their agricultural fields. In this way these two classes i.e., the peasant castes like *Jethoras*, and *Thakurs*, and the traders—the Bhotias, developed a symbiotic relationship with each other. The peasant castes become the tenants of the Bhotias' lands of the 'pattis' of *Goriphat* and *Talla Johar:* Since the regions of Malla Johar are exclusively inhabited only by Bhotias, for the exploitation of the agricultural lands of this region, the Bhotias depended on their low caste servants such as, Shilpkar and Kunkiya families, who were entirely dependent upon the rich Bhotias for thier subsistence. In this way, it is found that, the Bhotias carried out trade and agriculture simultaneously, the trade as the main occupation and agriculture as the subsidiary occupation.

LAND TENURE SYSTEM IN BHOTIA REGION

The trader Bhotias and their relationship with the peasant castes for the land exploitation purposes gave birth to a variety of proprietory right or tenureship on lands. In the Bhotia region, there have been the following types of land ownership and proprietory rights.

HISSEDAR

Hissedars have been those people who were the original proprietors and cultivators of land when the British took possession of the region from Gurkhas. At present they are the owners of the land they possess.

KHAIKAR

Khaikars are those people who cultivated lands in village owned by people of other villages and were the *hissedars.* But the rights of these people on such lands are hereditary except that they have to pay a certain amount as tax, known as *Malikana,* to the owners over and above the land revenue paid to the Government. There were two types of *khaikars—'Pakka'* and *'Kachcha' Khaikars. 'Pakka Khaikars'* were the cultivators of those land in the village which was owned by the *Hissedars* of the other villages. When the cultivator was exploiting the land of the *Khaikar*, he was known as *Kachcha Khaikar.*

The *Khaikars* (tenants) also have headman (in their stratum of right—Powel, 1974) called *'ghar-pradhan'*, and when the land lord is non-resident, the *'ghar-pradhan'* manages the village. The *Khaikars,* thus, form a class of 'occupancy-tenants' on a natural tenure, and no others are known.

SIRTAN

Sirtans are the tenants. Labourers called in to help are *'Sirtan'*, they are *tenant-at-will,* it may happen that a Khaikar of one village will cultivate land in another village as a *Sirtan.* The *Sirtans* may pay to the proprietors in cash or kind e.g., half of the yield or one third of the yield. A *Sirtan* can be tenant of a *Hissedar* or *Khaikar.*

The right in land is called *'thaat'*, and the proprietors "*thatwaan*". In the Bhotia region, the settled peasants are mostly the tenant cultivators and the owner cultivators.

Until 1960 the tenant-owner relationship between the peasants and the Bhotia traders went on smoothly. But, after the enactment of the Zamindari Abolition Act, 1960, there has been a drastic change in the land-holding pattern of the Bhotias. However, it will be discussed in the subsequent chapters.

PASTORALISM

Pastoralism has been closely related to the Bhotia's trade economy. In the rugged and inhospitable terrain of the trans and sub-Himalayan region, until recently, all dry commodities and such articles as grain, salt, and wool, were being transported from one place to another by the sure-footed animals like the sheep, goat, jibu, and ponies. These animals travelled through the narrow tracks or the goat tracks to the different places situated at varying altitudes.

For the Bhotia traders, the animals like sheep, goats, ponies, yaks, jibus, have been of immense use. These animals have played a diversified role in the economic structure of the Bhotias. While the cows were kept as milchcattle and the ponies used in the shaddle, the sheep, goats, jibu, yak or the mules mainly served as beasts of burden, and were also put to' another uses such as the jibus and bullocks as drought animals for ploughing ; the sheep for obtaining wool. the goat for getting mutton, etc.

Sheep and goats have, by far, been the most important livestock of Bhotias. Pant (1935) says, "His (Bhotia) survival is entirely dependent upon the goats and sheep which supply him not only with his daily meat but also with his attire and bedding. The hair and wool is used for the making of tents, ropes, bags, and garments. When alive they are used as beasts of burden and provide him with wool, and when they are dead their hides, furs, sinews, and bones are used as household furniture or sold for cash. They are in short, the Bhotias' mainstay". The importance of livestock among Bhotias has been so much that richness among them is often measured by the strength of the flock. Above all, it was on these animals that a Bhotia relies for the mobility which has been an essential part of his life.

The cattle wealth of Bhotias, in fact, have been an essential adjunct to their semi-nomadic life and trade economy. Besides facilitating their migratory operations, the cattle-wealth of the Bhotias helped them in transporting the items of export and import. All exportable goods, collected right from the terai market centres and sub-Himalayan trading centres, were transported to the trans-Himalayan region—Tibet after loading them on the animals. Similarly, the items of import like salt, borax wool, etc. were being brought in India by loading them on the Bhotias' animals. Besides facilitating their own migration and trade, the Bhotias also used them for transporting the commodities of the hill people.

Though Bhotias depended heavily upon their cattle wealth, they never acted as cattle breeders. Most of their cattles belonged to Tibetan stock which they used to buy or exchange for different goods. For grazing these animals, Bhotias used to employ servants who are known as 'Anwal'. But the poor Bhotia families used to graze their cattle by themselves. Some Bhotia families, who were not economically well-off, were earning their livelihood by grazing the rich Bhotia's cattle. These cattle were grazed in different pasture lands. While in Tibet, the graziers used to take them to the Tibetan pastures, and when in Malla Johar, the pasture land was available only in the alpine zones. During the summer the Bhotias' cattle were being grazed in the alpine pasture, and in the winter, the forest of the terai regions near Ramnagar, Nainital, and Tanakpur, were frequented for grazing them. Johari Bhotias call their male sheep and goats as '*Mena*' and '*Bahri*' respectively. The female sheep and goats are called as '*Kashili*'. Goats are considered to be more fit than sheep for carrying weight. A young goat carries about 10-12 kg. of weight and walks aoout 8-10 kms. a day. But a sheep carries only 5-6 kg. of weight and covers a distance of 4-5 kms a day. The 'he' goats and sheeps are sterolised in the infancy by castrating the testicles. The castrated goats and sheep not noly carry more weight but also produce more mutton. The food grains are first packed in a hemp-cloth bag known as *Karbas* and then loaded on the back of the pack animal. The 'Karbas' or saddlebag consists of two bags, joint together, and hang on each side of the pack animal's belly.

WOOLLEN INDUSTRY

Associated with trade, another element of the Bhotias' economy has been their woollen industry. The production of woollen goods is the only cottage industry of the Bhotias, and they enjoy a good reputation as being the fine weavers of woollen yarn into beautiful garments and textures. Wool spinning and weaving is a part of every day routine in a Bhotia family and all members of the family participate in spinning.

In their trade with Tibet, Bhotia, besides importing a variety of articles, imported a large amount of wool. The cold climate and the luscious grass make the wool of Tibet highly suitable for finer stuffs. The fleeces of the sheep and goats bred in the trans-Himalayan are very strong and long-stapled. Hence, the Bhotias imported huge quantities of Tibetan wool, for their own clothes, and for the costlier home spun products made for sale. During their trade with Tibet, wool formed the chief article of import. While a major part of the imported wool was being sold out to the Kanpur mills, Bhotias retained a select quantity of wool for their own use, from which home spun products were manufactured for self-use and marketing.

It generally happened that while the Bhotia men were engaged in the trans-Himalayan or submontane trip for effecting trade transactions, their women stayed at home, either in the higher settlements or in the valleys. Being left alone, and having abundant leisure at their disposal, they developed a special aptitude for spinning and weaving wool into beautiful and durable fabrics, and also for seeking ampler life in clubs and guilds. These tendencies primarily got encouraged by the abundance of raw wool yielded by their flocks, both indigenous and Tibetan, and by their proximity to the Tibetan wool-marts.

The Bhotias generally employed three varieties of row wool, according to the species of goats and sheep available. For coarse woollen blankets, ropes, and bags, they used the shearings of cis-Himalayan or Kumaon-bred carrier-goats and sheep. For ordinary medium-grade products, the wool of the *byun*, or the flocks set aside for the propagation, was utilized. And, for exceptionally fine products the *pushm* wool was used.

For spinning the sheared wool it is first soaked in hot water, beaten, and washed. The wool is spun generally by menfolk into different grades of yarn. While the men spin, women weave. The spinning is done by hand or with the manually operated spinning wheel known as Charkha. For spinning with hand, a simple hand-spindle known as .'*takli*' or '*Katwa*' is used. It consists of a little bamboo stick to the bottom of which a small round weight is affixed. A circular block of wood, 1.1/2 inches in diameter, is pierced through the centre with a bamboo spindle no thicker than an ordinary black-lead pencil and 6 to 9 inches in length. The Bhotia keeps his spindle twirling all day long and especially when the flocks are being driven along the roads, or when he is sitting by the fireside. Talking about the Bhotias' spinning skill Pant (1935) says, "he is always busy with his spindle or katwa during his marching hours, or when he is tending flocks in the forest. His assuidity is so great that he walks with one eye on his laden goats and one on the spindle. He is always to be seen with a skein of wool, which he carries on his wrist like a bracelet, and he goes on spinning even while talking, walking, sitting, or carrying a load".

The yarn spun by Bhotias is of two types, *viz.* single-play yarn for coarse textures, when the raw wool is spun into yarn by applying torsion anti-clockwise, and two-play yarn for closer textures, when two singleplay threads are combined by applying a clock-wise torsion. The yarn, when spun, is not directly sold, but is woven into fabrics. Unlike the Jaad Bhotias, Johari Bhotia spinners are also their own weavers. The male preponderance of spinners is more than counterbalanced by the women weavers. The chief occupation of women has been weaving, besides, of-course, the household work. The looms (*Raanch*), on which the Bhotia women weave the woollen fabrics, are simple and primitive. It consists of ten or twelve small sticks and a few cords and leather straps fitted in a rectangular wooden frame.

The Johari Bhotias have earned a great reputation as weavers. Nowhere else in the district of Pithoragarh and in the whole of Kumaon is such a combination of advantages as regards raw material and human aptitude to be found. Nowhere else the woollen industry, as of Bhotias, is so inextricably interwoven with the hole texture of domestic and social life. The Bhotias have become specialised and celebrated throughout the region for manufacturing the woollen materials like *thulma* (blankets), *pattus* (coarse woollen serge), *pankhis* (woollen, wrapper), *chutka* (a thick woollen blanket or coarse rug), *dann* (carpet), *asan* (prayer rug), etc.

'*Thulma*' is a thick woollen blanket, either black or white, according to the natural colour of the wool. It is first made in the form of a coarse woollen serge and then in the last three or four coarse serge are sewn together to make the blanket. After weaving it is flurred and then combed. Combing is done with sharp bamboo needles, fastened together like a broom. This is a very delicate task, and the value of the blanket or thulma depends on the successful results of the combing. Usually six to eight days are required for the manufacture of a *thulma.* Some 5 to 10 Kgs. of wool go to the making of one blanket. The black *thulmas* are costlier than the white ones. The Johari Bhotias excel the Bhotias of other valleys in combing and weaving this type of blanket.

'*Pankhis*' are coarse, warm woollen wrappers. They are seldom coloured. Two to three widths are stiched together to form a *pankhi.* Sometimes they are of single thickness, sometimes of double. Pankhis are lighter in weight than the thulmas, and are generally used to those people who cannot afford the costlier products. One singlesheet wrapper or pankhi is manufactured in three days.

'*Chutkas*' are thick coarse rugs with long hair loosely woven in the midst of the yarn. The hairy side of the *chutkas* looks like the fleece of a goat, and the other side is plain and even. The size of the chutka is similar to that of a *thulma*, but the cost is somewhat less.

'*Danns*' are small pile carpets, usually the size of a dressing table or a cot. These carpets are embellished by the designs in various colours. The Bhotias have successfully copied or imitated the Tibetan designs, which are interesting and consistent, but, unlike the Tibetans, they fail to match the colours. The yarn is washed and dyed before weaving. Formerly the dyes were prepared with the vegetable products of the region (Mainly 'akhrot') but recently aniline dyes have begun to replace those natural dyes. The danns are used for spreading over the cots, bedding, and for sitting in the sunshine during the winter.

'*Asans*' or prayer rugs are generally square. Their length is just half that of the danns, and in design and weave they follow them closely. They are used by the hill people as prayer carpets, and cost from Rs. 20 to Rs. 50.

The marketing of these woollen materials are generally done in the trade fairs like Jauljibe-Fair, Thal-Fair, and Bageshar-Fair. But the customers of these woollen products even approach Bhotias personally and obtain them on cash payment from their villages.

4

Trade and Old Social Order

It is no doubt true that environment of a man plays on important role in determining the course of his socio-cultural life. But, equally important is the influence of man on the environment. In fact, man and his environment are interrelated and both influence each other in different ways and degrees. The peculiar life style of Bhotias bears a clearcut impact on the environment. But besides environment, the other important factor which has greatly influenced the Bhotias' socio-cultural life is their economy. The economy of the Bhotias', which has been primarily dependant on the Indo-Tibetan or the trans-Himalayan trade, has had considerable influence on their social life. The settlement pattern, semi-nomadic and transhumance life, household management pattern, family, social interaction pattern, etc. of Bhotias have been an adjunct and a coefficient to their trading economy.

In the present chapter, it has been discussed that how the different elements of Bhotias' social life have been correlated with the principal element of their economic system i.e., the Indo-Tibetan trade. The chapter which follows this will examine cumulative effect on the different elements of Bhotias' socio-cultural life caused by the sudden gust of change in principal element of economy or by the stoppage of the Indo-Tibetan trade.

SETTLEMENT PATTERN

The mobility forced upon the Bhotia traders by the climate and environment has led to a proliferation of dwellings, each inhabited by a certain times of the year and adopted to specific uses. In the Bhotia region we can distinguish between three types of permanent settlements viz., *Summer settlement* or *main villages, Winter settlement,* and *Intermediate* or *Enroute Settlement.* The life of the Johari Bhotias has been made up of regular and successive changes of place. It alternated between permanent and temporary habitations, according to the cycle of the seasons. It has been intimately connected with the proximity of permanent inhabitations, and with the existence of pasture lands which are dependant upon geographic conditions and the seasons. All this, naturally, have had long established customs, traditions,and superstitions which also formed the chief means of social control.

Almost all the summer habitations or settlements are situated in the high and cold valleys towards the Tibetan frontier, where climate from May to September is very invigorating. Milam, Mertoli, Burfu, Lwan, and Pachchu are some of the villages of the summer settlement of Johari Bhotias. These villages served as bases for the Bhotias' Tibetan trade, and as depot and stores for the exports to Tibet. It was in these Himalayan residences that the Bhotia women and children with their milch cattle were left, when their menfolk were engaged in frequenting the Tibetan markets during the months of July to September. The villages of the summer settlement of Bhotias are also their main or original villages, and it has been customary among these people to derive the name of their clans or endogamous groups from these villages. These villages are situated between elevations of 3500 and 4500 metres from the sea level.

In the winter, when the higher valleys are blocked with snow, the rigour of the climate always compelled the Bhotias to descend in warmer and more convenient localities such as Tejam, Kwity, Timitia, Thal and Bhainskhal. These villages are situated in the river valleys lying between 1500 and 2500 metres. Since these villages are inhabited during winter, they form the *winter settlement* of the Johari Bhotias. The Bhotia families resided here from November to March.

Besides these two settlements, which are also common among the other Bhotia groups, the Johari Bhotias maintained one additional set of settlement known as *Intermediate* or *Enroute Settlement*. As the name signifies, the Intermediate settlement of the Johari Bhotias is situated in between the two main settlements, i.e., the summer and winter settlements. Malla Dummer, Darkot, Suring, Jalath, Daranthi and Gorpatha are some of the villages of the Intermediate settlement. These villages are situated at the elevations of 1800 to 3000 metres and are resided for only one to two months, i.e., April and May. In this settlement too the Johari Bhotias have got their permanent dwellings. All these three set of settlements are equipped with different sets of utensils, bedding, homestead materials, etc. in the case of the rich members of the community, but in the case of the poorer ones everything is carried up and down when the migrations take place.

As mentioned earlier, the villages of summer settlement are also the main villages of the Johari Bhotias. Each village of this settlement was occupied by one distinct clan or exogamous groups of Bhotias. While the members of one clan or exogamous group of Johari Bhotias have been concentrated in one village of the summer settlement, in the winter and intermediate settlements the clan members did not concentrate in any one village. Instead, there they got proliferated and dispersed in more than one villages. While in most of the cases these villages too remained uniclan villages, some Bhotia villages also developed in the form of multiclan villages. Ghorpatta, Choribagar, Daranthi, etc. are some of the multi-clan villages of the Intermediate settlement. Again it is seen that while most villages of summer settlement are single ethnic group Bhotia village, barring some low caste or shilpkar families who have been dependent upon Bhotias for their subsistence, the villages of winter and intermediate settlements are multi-ethnic group of mixed villages and are also inhabited by the people of caste groups like Rajput, Brahman, Jethora, and Shilpkar. But, in the mixed Bhotia village the dwellings of the Bhotias are clustered in the centre whereas those of the caste groups are in the periphery.

From the Table 6 we can see the distribution of Bhotia clan in the villages of their all the three settlements.

SEMINOMADISM AND TRANSHUMANCE

The entire Bhotia culture area falls under the greater Himalayan system and is characterized by its physiographic diversities. The irregularities in relief and variations of the altitude of the mountain ranges give rise to great contrast in the climatic conditions within short distances. In the higher valleys, the winters are severe as compared to the lower valleys and thus the Bhotias are forced to descend to the lower valleys. This kind of movement, due to the environmental conditions, has been a culture trait of the Bhotias and it is one of the characteristic features of their adjustment with the physical environment.

The seasonal movement of the Bhotias has been a combination of semi-nomadism and transhumance because they had to resort to a temporary migration enmasse from their permanent villages at higher altitudes due to the severity of climate and shortage of pasture for the cattle. But apart from climate and pastoralism, a trade has been an important factor in making the Bhotias a semi-nomadic people. Rawson (1963) remarked that, "their (Bhotias) nomadism was mainly related with their occupation, i.e., the Tibetan trade". Similarly, Spate (1954) observed, "at the highest level live the Bhotias, among whom pastoralism and trading are more important than agriculture.

TABLE 6

Distribution of Bhotia Clans in the Villages of Their Three Sets of Settlements

Serial No.	*Bhotia Clans*	*Bhotia Village in the :*		
		Summer Settlement	*Intermediate Settlement*	*Winter Settlement*
1	2	3	4	5
1.	Rawat	Milam	Jallath	Kwity, Tejam, Lachuli
2.	Pangtey	Milam	Darkot	Bhainskhal, Bhainskot
3.	Dhamsatu	Milam	Darkot	Timtia, Kanauli
4.	Nikhurpa	Milam	Nanasem	—
5.	Burfal	Burfu	Daranthi	Kolia, Pamtori
6.	Jangpangi	Burfu	Malla Dummer	Mawani, Bamori, Susket
7.	Lowal	Lowa	Jallath, Talla Dummer	Jhalori
8.	Panchpal	Pachchu	Talla Ghorpatta	Simgiri
9.	Mapwal	Mapa	Ranthi	—
10.	Mertolia	Mertoli	Suring, Malla Ghorpatta, Mina	Timla Bagar, Devibaga

(1)	(2)	(3)	(4)	(5)
11.	Biljuwal	Bilju	Talla Dummer, Ghorpatta	Simgiri
12.	Tolia	Tola	Sainpolu, Thankhdhura	Simgiri
13.	Sumdyal	Sumdu	Ranthi	——
14.	Ghangharia	Ghanghar	Talla Ghorpatta	Thala
15.	Rilkotia	Rilkot	Dhapa	——
16.	Laspal	Laspa	Kuiri-Jimia	——
17.	Khinchiyal	Khelanch	Shela	——

Of these 17 Bhotia clans, the first four clans are collectively known as Milmals due to residing in one common village Milam. Earlier these four clans were one and did not marry each other. But due to the demographic reasons, these clans got split up into four different exogamous clans.

Their alpine pasture lie at 10,000-13,000 feet in valleys with little rain but much winter-snow."

Carrier (1932) has made a distinction between the 'greater transhumance' and 'lesser transhumance'. Greater transhumance is that which involves movements between a mountain region and its surrounding lowlands or plateaus, whereas lesser transhumance is that which includes movement within the mountain region from lower to higher slope. A study of the transhumance practices among the Johari Bhotias discloses that their seasonal movement has been a peculiar blend of greater and lesser transhumance. These periodic migrations have resulted also, besides trade, from the necessity of finding new pastures and ensuring a regular food supply to the cattle or beasts of burden.

Thus it is evident that the seasonal movements in permanent settlements and transhumance of Bhotias have been related, besides the climatic factor, with their trading and pastoral economy which, in turn, were also interrelated. Now, it will be seen that how actually the course of Bhotias' semi-nomadic and pastoral life was being determined by their trade and pastoral economy.

There have been three distinct varieties of migrations among the Bhotias. In the first, only the carrier-flocks and traders moved ; in their second, the families accompanied their traders and their flocks, and in the third, herds of cattle were moved in charge of three or four graziers, and accommodated in the '*buygal*'. Following is the order in which these migrations took place :

April-May	First upward trip of traders with goat and mules
May-June	Traders'-second trip
Mid June	Families with '*jibus*', etc.
June-July	Camp followers consisting of tenants, doms or shilpkars.
Mid September	First downward trip.

End of September Second downward trip
October Families descended

The traders with the carrier-flocks remained on the move throughout the year, except for a brief period during the summer and winter. In addition to escorting their families, they went to Tibet and the markets of the 'terai' regions.

Immediately after the middle of April, when the trade fair at Thal was over, the Bhotia traders used to start on their upward march towards the higher camps, their flocks hoving been laden with cereals, such as rice, mandua, and barley ; luxuries such as tea, cloth, brass, and copper wares, etc. The flocks consisting chiefly of goats and sheep, which usually carried gain. The richer traders, however, used hardier and more expensive animals : mules, 'jibus', and ponies, etc, carried heavier commodities. The usual caravan of an ordinary Bhotia well-to-do family consisted of 100 to 125 goats and sheep, 10 to 12 mules and 'jibu' 3 to 5 ponies.

The merchandise was first stored in the Intermediate settlement of the Johari Bhotias. When all the goods were thus brought up from the submontane markets, preparations were made, after a brief sojourn in the Intermediate settlement, for shifting them to the villages of upper residences or summer settlement. But, before venturing to move enmasse, a pilot party was sent to repair the crude bridges and paths that might have been damaged by the action of the ice and snow during the past winter. When the road leading to the upper-settlement and passes had been cleared then the flocks which brought the goods from the lower regions were laden once more, but this time the lightly, on account of the hazardous and fatiguing nature of the track. After reaching the upper habitations the goods, which worth thousands, were stored in the villages, and then the traders used to return without leaving any guard to watch them. This carelessness was possible because nature has provided peculiar safegurds.

Immediately after the completion of the transportation of merchandise goods, preparations were made for the larger and more difficult migration. In this phase of migration, the entire families with cattle, bag and baggage moved. Though this migration has been full of ordeals, it provided a spectacle full of interest and beauty. During this migration whole villages were seen on the move, with women and children, old and young, infirm and healthy, cattle and dogs, all on the trek to their dwellings. An auspicious day was fixed by the village astrologer. Usually the villagers belonging to the same territory marched together. The three or four days before the up-hill journey have always been very busy. Both men and women were engaged in packing the goat bags (Karbas) with grain. All the surplus utensils, bedding, and supply of food were sorted out and put safely on one side, and the things to be carried up were selected and packed. While the goats and sheep started a day earlier with the shepherds (anwal), the other pack-animals like ponies, 'jibus', etc, accompanied the Bhotia families. The head of the family or the leader of the caravan, used to leave last of all. He was supposed to lead the ponies and 'jibus' and lock up the house, look carefully to ensure that nothing had been left behind, that everything had been packed and dispatched.

Usually, the upward march used to start at four in the morning. The children in arms were carried in a cylindrical basket (Doka). Women without children used to carry in their basket or 'doka' the articles like wine, broom, pots and pans and cups, sickle, etc. Besides the 'doka' or back-pack basket, a small hand basket (functa) was carried by the women. The 'functa' contained the tiffin, toilet articles-comb and oil flask, medicines, butter, a hand spindle (katwa), and wool. These last two articles have been indispensable, owing to the industrious character of the people, who invariably spin as they plodded along with the caravan.

The whole party, after covering 3 to 8 miles, depending upon the strength of its members, used to halt around nine O' clock at some convenient level spot. Here the tent (tarkeb) which weighed about 6 Kgs. was erected by means of poles which was improvised on the spot. A Bhotia 'tarkeb, could accommodate a family of five. The richer Bhotia families however, used the 'tambu', which is more elaborate and heavier and more spacious. In an encampment of forty to fifty 'tarkebs' only four or five 'tambus' were found. The poorest class of migrant sought shelter in the rock-shelters (udyar). Next morning, after first day's halt, the camp was again dislodged for further journeys. This daily routine of making a new camp was continued until the summer habitiations were reached.

On reaching the highest Himalayan settlements, all the animals, carriers and otherwise were sent in charge of a few herdsmen to the 'bugyal' (pasture). The pack-animals were brought back from the 'bugyal' to the trade depots after a fortnight or a month's grazing, and packed again for going to Tibet for effecting trade transactions.

The further marches into Tibet were undertaken immediately the trade passes were open, sometimes in the end of June and batch of traders used to cross the border lines between the 1st and 15th July. The migration into Tibet was attended with more ceremony than the other marches. The march was usually undertaken after the *Haryala* festival was over. The night previous to the departure was spent in worships of the Gods, in preparing rich dishes, and providing rations for the journey. Tibet, being a bleak and barren country, affords very meagre facilities for the provision and cooking of the daily means. Hence, to ensure against starvation, such a provision as cooked food was made as it would have lasted throughout the march, and would not deteriorate by keeping. The principal rations were parched rice, flour, boiled meat and tobacco. The following morning all the men, women, and children marched off together to the accompaniment of music. The women and children accompanying the departing traders used to escort them as far as some watering-place like spring, stream, or pond. Generally the watering place lie a mile from the settlement, and here they have had erected a temple. The final scene used to be extremely pathetic. Every man bound for Tibet used to clasp his dear ones to his breast, and all the women and children were in tears.

Usually two trips to Tibet were undertaken. The first was over by the end of July, and the flocks used to return with wool, rugs and skins. Much of the spinning and weaving work in the highest habitations awaited the arrival of this wool which, when brought to the village, was cleaned and spun by womenfolk. The second trip usually was finished by the end of August or the begining of September, the bigger traders remaining in Tibet as late as October. After a fortnight's rest, preparations were afoot for the downward marches, and by the end of October the highest habitational sites were completely deserted, all activity being transferred to submontane bases.

After the settlement in their sub-Himalayan residences, the Bhotia traders used to undertake further trips, this time to the *Bhabar markets* for example Ramnagar, and Haldwani passing through Almora or Ranikhet ; the richer traders used to pay one visit to some large centre, such as Delhi, Amritsar, Calcutta, Bhagalpur or Bombay. Between September and April two trips were usually made for the Bhabar or terai markets where all the wool was disposed off.

From the above discussion, it is amply clear that the trade and pastoral economy of the Bhotias led them to lead a seminomadic and transhumant life. While their Indo-Tibetan trade necessiated them to make seasonal and successive uphill and down-hill migrations, the search of green pastures for the cattle or pack-animals, gave birth to a transhumance activities among them.

FAMILY AND HOUSEHOLD ORGANIZATION

Family is the basic social group and forms the first sphere in which individuals combine. The base of family is quite often rooted in social and economic conditions, when considered from a cultural point of view. In this study, the family of the Bhotias has been studied from the cultural point of view and an attempt has also been made to find out as to what extent the social and economic conditions have influenced the structure and organization of the Bhotia's family.

In such an investigation, it is quite imperative to keep in mind the natural environment because it plays a vital role in determining the structure of the family, besides several other cultural elements. In all cases the form and size of the social group, the nature of its activities, the trend and limit of its development will be strongly influenced by the size and nature of its habitat. The social and economic factors are closely related to the environmental conditions. Fuchs (1947) remarks that, "the social organisation of a tribe is strongly influenced by the economic life it leads and also by the natural environment in which it lives". The environment indirectly influences the form of family, though its rate of influence varies according to the cultural environment.

The limited environmental possibilities compelled the inhabitants of the Bhotia region to resort to a distinct" type of economy for their livelihood. They are traders, herdsmen, craftsmen, as well as agriculturists. The climate induced in them a seasonal rhythm which has been reflected in their migratory characteristics. Due to the diverse economic and climatic conditions, their families share the characteristics of the family system of both the primitive agriculturists and the pastoral nomads. In the traditional Bhotia society, *joint* family has been a rule rather than exception. The family consists of parents, sons and their wives and children. They all share the common household and help each other in household as well as outside work. More often, co-operation ends when the joint families break up on the death of the head of the family.

In order to meet their diverse requirements, Bhotias practice various types of occupations side by side. All this, naturally sought for a large number of persons in the each household. Hence, their economy forced them to live in a *joint family*, quite often supplemented by *extended family*.

The male and female have equal status in the family and have a different code of duties to perform. The importance and status of women however in the family here has been greater than elsewhere. Spate (1955) remarks, "a notable contrast with the rest of the Kumaon is provided by the higher and more independent status of the Bhotia women, left for long spells incharge of home and field, with only the children and the aged to help them. Environmental factors in this situation are not so far to seek, though Mongolian affinities are probably also responsible in part". The male members had to live outside for trade and for rearing sheep and goats in the pastures, for the greater part of the year. Hence women have had to attend the varied works from preparing meals to managing outside affairs. They prepare meals, grind the grains, clean the cattle-shed, and collect the fodder and fuel from the jungle. Pant (1935), in his pioneering work on the Social Economy of Himalayas, has rightly remarked about the role and status of Bhotia women in the Bhotia Society. He says, "among the Bhotias the women occupy an important place. All the able-bodied males migrate during the summer months to Tibet, and during the winter to submontane marts, leaving everything in charge of the women. During this period they have to manage all the domestic affairs of the community, and sometimes tackle difficult problems and take important decisions on their own initiative. This training in responsibility makes them self-reliant and capable housewives".

Besides these duties, a Bhotia woman also performs the work of agriculture, except ploughing which is done by men. In her spare time, a Bhotia woman occupies herself with spinning and weaving, the main cottage industry of the Bhotias and main stay of their winter trade with Tibet. Hence, the position of women in the Bhotia family has been quite high and important. It had resulted into an equal relationship of husband wife in the family. The interference of women in the outer task has made them bold and self-sufficient and industrious. Mazumdar (1958) remarks that, "the economic independence of Bhotia women has given them considerable freedom in social and economic life".

But the pattern of family life and household organization has undergone considerable changes due to the dynamics of transformation in the main element of their economic system. However, it will be examined in the subsequent chapter.

SOCIAL STRATIFICATION

Bhotia society is a rank stratified society. It is divided into three distinct social classes which are also endogamous. The social classes in Bhotia society are related with a highly differentiated economy and, to some extent, also with the concept of ritual pollution. Among the Johari Bhotias, the three ranked social classes, which parallels the hierarchic order characteristic of Hindu society, are known as *Bharet*, *Kunkiya*, and *Nitwal*. However, the overwhelming majority of Johari Bhotias belongs to the *Bharet* class. A brief description about these three classes will show that how the trading economy, which helped Bhotias to a mass wealth, led to the formation of status groups.

BHARET

Bharet is the elite class of the Bhotia Society. Bhotias belonging to this class are not only economically well-off, but also enjoy a superior ritual and ethnic status. Ritual and ethnic superiority is claimed in terms of having a determined ancestral and marital bonds. The Bharet Bhotias have been successful and prosperous traders. But all Bharet Bhotias did not command equal socio-economic status. Even among the Bharet Bhotias, there has always been some leading Bharet clans. *Rawat*, *Jangpangi*, *Pangtey*, *Mertolia Tolia* and few others have been the economically dominant Bharet clans of Johari Bhotias. The Bhotias of these clans have earned great reputation as successful and rich traders. People of these clans have not only been economically dominant, but even numerically more significant than others. These Bharet clans and some rich Bhotia families of other clans too, in order to show their superior Socio-Economic Status over others, kept some servants for doing various jobs. For doing odd jobs they kept '*Kunkiyas*', whereas for cooking food, '*Nitwals*' were employed by them. With the passage of time, these peoples got associated with such clans and became an inseparable part from the Bhotia Society. But these two groups, who are primarily functional groups, correspond to different social status and have a separate identity in terms of their ritual and ethnic status.

KUNKIYAS

Kunkiya is an inferior class in the stratified society of Bhotias. Kunkiyas are like servants meant primarily for doing odd jobs like carrying household articles during migration, grazing the flocks, collecting firewoods, washing dirty clothes, etc. They were earlier known as '*Kanchukiyas*' and were bought and sold like slaves. Traditionally, Kunkiyas are linked with almost all the Johari Bhotia clans, depending on the individual family's economic strength, and are recognized after the name of the Bhotia clan with whom they are attached. They are quite often referred to as 'Rawat Ka Kunkiya' (Rawat clan's Kunkiya), 'Pangtey Ka Kunkiya', and so on. Sometime these Kunkiyas enjoy their superior status among themselves by linking them with rich Bharet Bhotia clans. For example, the Rawat's Kunkiya enjoys greater social status than the Tola's Kunkiya. Like Bharet Bhotias, Kunkiya Bhotias, are endogamous and hence marry only among themselves.

In day to day behaviour the distinctions between Bharet Bhotias and Kunkiya Bhotias are not apparent to the casual visitor to a Johari Bhotia village. But, after a detailed observation such differences are easily discenible. Bharet Bhotia makes no distinction with Kunkiya Bhotias in terms of inter-dining and ordinary social inter-course. But on social ceremonies and communal feasts, they were not allowed to sit in a row and eat food in the utensils made of bronze. Among the Johari Bhotias, besides the Kunkiyas of different Bhotia clans, there are some recognized and independent Kunkiya groups. Such Kunkiya groups are known as *'Hamjali'*, *Kurial*, *Lowal*, and *Gamswal*. Besides those Kunkiya groups, however, there are, in general, the following types of Kunkiya Bhotias:

1. *Bharet Kunkiyas*

Some of the rich Bhotias of bygone days, who were known as Bharets, could not retain their economic prosperity in the trade markets and thus lost their socio-economic position. Due to economic backwardness, such Bharets could not obtain spouses from among the rich Bharet people. Under such circumstances, they were compelled to seek spouses from the outside people, and thus they brokeup the rule of endogamy. The Bharet Bhotias, who due to their economic reasons, married outside community, were socially cutcasted and labelled as Kunkiyas. This category of Kunkiyas, who were earlier Bharets, are locally known as ***Rajpa***, ***Dhopa***, and *Namjali*.

IMMIGRANT KUNKIYAS

Immigrant Kunkiyas are of two types—

(1) *Garhwali Immigrant*, and (2) *Khasia Kunkiyas*.

Some people, who were economically well-off and commanded high social status came to Johar valley from Garhwal for trading purposes and got settled. But they could not complete with the Bhotia traders and lost their socio-economic position. In such a situation they established affinal relationship with the Bharet-Kunkiyas and thus got assimilated in the

Bhotia society. But, they also were labelled as Kunkiyas. Such Kunkiyas locally are known as *Miria*, and *Gamswal*.

Similarly, some Khasia people knowing, '*Tantras*' and '*Mantras*' came to Johar valley for exploring the prospect of earning livelihood. They were highly fascinated with the scenic beauty of Johar valley and got settled over there by marrying the Kunkiya girls. This category of Kunkiyas are known as *Dubaria*, *Bam* and *Mahar*.

Though there are different types of Kunkiyas in the Bhotia society, but the main Kunkiyas are those who were engaged by Bharet Bhotias as their servants. The Kunkiya Bhotias and their family members were totally dependent on the Bharet Bhotia for their subsistence and sustenance. The Bharet Bhotias used to give them, besides two time's meal, clothes, some unirrigated lands, few sheep and goats, etc. for pulling on their life somehow. To put in differently, the Kunkiya Bhotias have been more or less like a parasite on the Bharet Bhotias.

NITWALS

Like Kunkiyas, Nitwals also are the servants of Bharet Bhotias. But unlike Kunkiyas, the Nitwal Bhotias command higher ritual and occupational status. Instead of doing the odd jobs, Nitwal served as cooks (Rasoiya) and priests of the Bharet Bhotia. Almost every well-to-do Bharet Bhotia kept one Nitwal servant for cooking his food and performing the sacred rites and rituals. As a matter of fact, the Bharet Bhotias assigned a higher ritual status to the Nitwal Bhotias. The cooks of the Bhotias are called as Nitwal because these people have migrated from the Niti valley of Garhwal. The Nitwal Bhotias, due to their higher ritual status, abstain from eating the food cooked by Bharet and Kunkiya Bhotias. But this restriction is limited only for taking boiled food like rice, etc. They do not mind taking fried food like Puri, etc.

The Nitwal Bhotias, like Kunkiyas, have also been primarily dependent on Bharet Bhotias for their livelihood.

They did not go to Tibet for trade but instead did some cultivations in the agricultural fields given to them by the Bharets. Due to such economic dependence, the Nitwals and Kunkiyas have been leading a very hard and hand to mouth life. They had no autonomy over their own desires, social and economic activities. They have been fully exploited for a petty wages by the Bharet Bhotias. Most Kunkiya and Nitwal Bhotias, due to their total dependence on the rich and trader Bhotias, have remained innocent, ignorant, and illiterate. But with the change in the economic structure of the Bharet Bhotias, there has also been tremendous changes in the lifestyle and socio-economic conditions of these three social classes of the Johari Bhotia Society, which will be discussed in the subsequent chapter.

EXTERNAL SOCIAL RELATIONSHIP

The economic prosperity of the Bhotias, achieved primarily from their Indo-Tibetan trade in the District of Pithoragarh also resulted in the formation of a hierarchical order based on economic classes. The Bhotias became the highest of the social classes with their wealth, land, and also education. The caste groups of Bhotia regions were not only dependant on Bhotias for obtaining certain items imported from Tibet, but also got depended on their lands. They started exploiting their lands on share-crop basis and in the form of a *tenant-landlord* relationship. All this helped Bhotias in building a higher ritual status in the wider Hindu Society. However, the secular status system was reinforced gradually by a ritual hierarch too. This process of ritual status-acquirement was facilitated by their superior economic and political position. This resulted in their claiming the status of a Hindu Rajput caste in the caste hierarchy, though they remained endogamous as far as Rajputs of Kumaoni peasant society is concerned. The relationship of the Bhotia with the Brahman of lower status, especially in the Johar area, also developed into that of patron and client. Most

Bhotia families developed a traditional jajmani relationship with a certain Brahman family of that region. The lower caste who are collectively called as 'Shilpkars' in this area, were also brought within the structural interdependance of the Bhotia social structure. Thus, every Bhotia village has a number of shilpkar families of different occupational category attached to it. But after the stoppage of the Bhotias trader a significant change has occurred in the inter-caste inter-community relations of the Bhotia region. The dominant position of the Bhotias, economically as well as politically, could not be maintained. And, then the sub-ordinate groups like Kunkiyas, the shilpkars, Rajput and Brahmans, had to readjust their position vis-a-vis the Bhotias.

EDUCATION

Until the cessation of their Indo-Tibetan trade and being declared as Scheduled Tribe in the year 1967, Bhotias could not excel in the field of education. Their keen struggle for existence in the inhospitable environment and semi-nomadic life gave them little time to think for enlightenment through education. But, they never remained virtually illiterate. Barring the womenfolk, most Bhotia males took primary education. The economic struggle being their preoccupation, Bhotias mostly educated their sons only up to upper primary to up to middle class at the most. The only idea behind educating the sons was to enable them to carry on their ancestral trade efficiently. But even this much of education was limited among the Bharet Bhotias and rich traders, The Kunkiyas, Nitwals, and economically inferior Bhotias remained deprived from even the basic education. In general, during the trading economy of Bhotias, percentage of literacy among them have been deplorably low.

It was in the year 1890 when for the first time two Bhotia converts into Christianity, named Rev. Uttam Singh Rawat and Thakur Dalip Singh, went to Almora to study in the High School. Thakur Dalip Singh maintained his spirit for higher education and later on retired as Deputy Director in a Govt. department. Since then, i.e. from 1890, the urge for higher education has been sporadic. In Johar valley, there has been functioning some private and missionary schools which were taken by the District Board authorities in the year 1928.

Missionaries were the first to realise the need for education among the Johari Bhotias. First Primary School in village Milam was opened by the Missionary in the year 1904 which was followed by the opening of a school in the village Burfu by the *Zila Parishad* (District Board). The missionaries established schools and attempted to present at least rudimentary academic instruction in addition to the religious instruction. However, the Bhotias showed an indifferent attitude towards the religious preachings of the missionaries. In the beginning only boys were sent to the schools. Neither the education of girls was thought important nor they were sent in the school. It was mainly after 1930 that the pace of education among the Bhotias was slightly accelerated. Uptil 1950 or so, there was only one post graduate and 5 graduates in the Bhotia society.

No educated Bhotia was interested in going for the govt. services. They used to think it to be a derogatory work. It was held that by doing govt. and other services,there will be a decline in their socio-economie status which they have had gained through their dominant and thriving trade relations with Tibet. Hence, besides the general Bhotia tendency to indulge exclusively in their ancestral trading economy, even the educated Bhotias preferred to absorb themselves in the trading operations. But, after the closure of their trade and especially after gaining the status of a scheduled tribe in 1967, there has been a tremendous increase of education in the Bhotia society. Bhotias have become very much education consious and send all their children, irrespective of sex, for taking basic and higher education. The educated persons in the Bhotia society are getting inereasingly absorbed in govt. jobs which has made them a people of white collar jobs.

POLITICAL ORGANISATION

Until the middle of the nineteenth century, the Bhotia region was under the suzerainty of the Kirats, Chand Rajas, and Nepalis or Gorkhas. It was annexed to the British territory in the year 1815. Due to having a long spell of the external political influences, the Bhotias' socio-political life has seen many upheavals. Under the rule of different kings and political power, Bhotias had to observe a variety of principles in terms of maintaining social order, paying land revenue, etc. All this, naturally, have had considerable influence on the Bhotias' socio-political life.

The unit of the social control in the Bhotia society has been their village. Each village has had its headman who is traditionally known as PADHAN. In the Johar Valley where Bhotias inhabit, there has been 13 main villages of Bhotias and, hence, also 13 PADHANS. In the beginning a Padhan was selected either by nomination or direct selection by the ruling authorities of the region. Later on the post of the Padhan was made hereditary. Usually the most influential, educated and economically sound person was made the '*Padhan*'. In every Bhotia clan, which is based on the village inhabited by them, the 'Padhan' was generally selected from among the members of the seniormost lineage group or the stalistically most significant clan. Among the Milmal Bhotia clan, the Padhan is also known as '*BURRAH*' because he belongs to the '*Burrath*' lineage. For assisting the 'Padhan' in his work, some assistants were also made who were known as '*MANTRI*'. The number of 'MANTRI' generally varies from 2 to 4 persons.

The duties of the 'Padhan' mainly correspond to (i) Revenue Collection, (ii) Tax collection, (iii) Dispute Settlement, and (iv) Sacred performance. The 'Padhan' of the every village was supposed to collect the land revenue from each land holder.

The land revenue so collected was later on deposited with the Tehsildar of the region. Besides the land revenue, the 'Padhan' of every village used to collect the trade taxes from the Bhotia traders. The taxes collected were submitted with the Burrah of village who used to pay it to the Tibet Government's trade agent—'Jongpen' in the form *La-thal.* The 'Padhan' of the Bhotia villages was also concerned with the settlements of disputes like cattle theft, eve-teasing, girl elopement, trade jealousies, etc. Besides, all this the Padhan of the village was considered the sacred specialist, for he was the person who was responsible for appearing the village deity, arranging socio-religious ceremonies, offering sacrifices, etc. No religious function or ceremony was performed without the presence and guidance of the '*Padhan*'. The 'Padhans' of the Bhotia villages were seldom interested in doing the works other than those concerned with trade, and their own cultural traditions. The duties pertaining to the collection of land revenue, and other taxes were forcibly imposed upon them by the ruling authorities and Bhotias felt it obligatory to perform such duties. But these assignments, however, with the course of time became the prestige symbol of the Padhans of different clans and villages. But, after the closure of the trade, there has been a total disorganisation of the Bhotia village life which has affected the traditional political system of the Bhotias.

CO-OPERATIVE SOCIETIES

For the benefit of the public and upliftment of the particular Bhotia groups or clans, a number of co-operative societies or Sahkari Samities have been functioning in the Johari Bhotia society. In the year 1946 they opened a co-operative society known as '*Johar Sangh*' which was later on registered with the Government (no. 194). It was opened with the joint venture of all Bhotia class who contributed money to it. The main objective behind the opening of such a co-operative society was to make available the items of export at a cheaper and convenient dealings. The members of this society. Like Johar Sangh, all Bhotia class of 13 Johar villages were having their own independent co-operative societies which were known as Rawat Sahkari Samiti, Pangtey Sahkari Samiti, Jangpangi Sahkari Samiti, and so on. The members of each Bhotia clan, who were basically traders, used to put their share in the 'Samiti' for earning profit on interest on capital, and obtaining loan at the time of emergency. The proceeds of these Samitis and Sanghs were spent on the general welfare of the Bhotia and Bhotia class. Besides these co-operative societies, there have been '*Nitwal Sangh*' and '*Paikasht-Sangh*. As the name indicates, the 'Nitwal Sangh' was run by the Nitwal Bhotias and 'Paikasht Sangh,' by the Kunkiya Bhotias who are also known as Paikasht. Since the people of these two social classes were economically inferior, they maintained their own organisation to discuss their socio economic problems. They all contributed a fixed amount of monthly subscription for the maintenance of their organisation. The members of these two 'sanghs', i.e., the Nitwal Sangh and Paikasht Sangh, due to their economic backwardness, had decided among themselves that like their Bharet Bhotias, they will not take any bride price while marrying their daughters. The needy person was given financial and moral support by the members of this Sangh. Thus, it is clear that during their trading economy, Johari Bhotias maintained very organized socio-economic institutions and organisations. Their Sanghs and Samitis, have not been only an economic institution, but also a symbol of social solidarity.

RELIGION

The religious life of the Bhotias has been a peculiar blend of Lamaistic Buddhism, Hinduism, and Animism. Sherring (1906) has rightly remarked, "The Bhotias being mongolians, we should naturally expect them to have much in common with the Tibetan, especially in their religion, but the reverse is the case". Similar views have also been expressed by Atkinson (1882), who says, "In religion they (Bhotias) are professedly

Buddhists, but practically as much mixed in this respect now as in descent, and can hardly be said to belong to any particular religion". Due to their long established trade relations with the Tibetans, pahari peasants, and plain dwellers, the Bhotias have had ample opportunities of coming into contact with the Tibetan and the Pan-Indian belief systems. All this have had tremendous effect on the body of the Bhotias' religious beliefs and practices. They got influenced with the pecularities of the different religious cults and also incorporated them in the configuration of their own religious beliefs and practices. All this, naturally, made the Bhotia religion a congregation of syncretic cults. The syncretic religious cult of the Bhotias, which has its base in their trading economy, however, may be conceived under the following heads. But, while describing the religious beliefs and practices of Bhotias, special emphasis will be laid on those elements which are acculturated and have been more or less an adjunct to the trade economy.

INFLUENCE OF TIBETAN CULTS ON THE BHOTIAS' RELIGIOUS LIFE

The Bhotias used to make periodical journeys to Tibet for their economic pursuits. In carrying out the trade relations with the Tibetans, the Bhotias quite often came into contact with the Tibetan '*Lamas*' (monks) and were greatly influenced with their sermons, religious preachings, and medico-religious activities. Bhotias started treating the Tibetan Lamas as their family's and ceremonial priests. Lamas were called by the Bhotias to perform the birth ceremony, naming ceremony, death rites, etc. For the safety of the village and its inhabitants, the Bhotias need to construct or erect "*Mana Walls*" around their dwellings by fixing the stone boulders one over the other. The Tibetan Lamas used to engrave 'mantra' in the Tibetan script on the boulders used for constructing Mana walls. The mantra engraved in the boulders read like this—'*Om Mane Padme Hum*'. Even these days one can find the remnants of the Mana Walls in the dilapidated dwellings in the summer settlement of the Johari Bhotias. It was believed by the Bhotias that this mantra has great powers and shall protect us from the evil spirits and misfortunes in the trade markets, and natural calamities. It was held by them in great esteem and reverence so much that they used to write this mantra in their outer garmemts. While coming back from Tibet after effecting the trade transactions, the Tibetan Lamas used to bless and wish them a safe and nice journey. Besides the usual blessings, the Tibetan Lamas used to put a seal or mohar (stamp) of clay, known as GERU, on the backs of the sheep, goats, and mules. It was believed that such seals on the backs of the pack-animals would save them from disease, and wild animals.

The Bhotias were also greatly influenced with the dragons of the Tibetans which is the totem animal of the Tibetans. This symbol is found represented in the Bhotias' woollen handicrafts. Bhotias generally put the design of a draggon on the carpets (Dann) which they manufacture. A draggon designed carpet is locally known as '*Duk-Design*' and is taken with deep esteem and reverence.

Besides the existence of Mana-walls and DUK-carpets, the other elements which reflect the influence of the Tibetan's influence on the Bhotias' religious life, are the worshipping of the some Tibetan gods or deities like Laandey, Manhfaila, etc. by the Bhotias. Bhotia have also emulated the practice of doing '*Lamhshell*' for the propitiation of a deity. Lamhshell is the peculiar way of worshiping the deities in which the participants or devotees gather at a place, construct manawall and then make offering to the deities. The Bhotias, like the Tibetans, also offer '*Sattu*' (gram powder) to their deities. The offering of 'Sattu' by the Bhotias to their deities are not made for all their deities but particularly to those ones which have got Tibetan origin e.g., Laandey, Manhfaila, etc. Besides offering 'Sattu' while propitiating the deities of Tibetan origin, the Bhotias also offer distilled and fermented wine e.g., Chakti or Daru, Chhang, Taan, etc. which is a typical Tibetan style of worshiping a deity.

WORSHIP OF DEITIES

Bhotias of Johar Valley worship a number of deities. While there are certain deities which are collectively worshipped by the Bhotias as well as by the local Hindu caste population, some deities are exclusively worshipped by the individual Bhotia clans. A list of the common deities i.e., the details which are worshipped both by the Bhotias and the local Hindu caste, and the individual clan deities of the Bhotias is given in the Table 7.

TABLE—7

List of Deities

Sl.	Common Deities	Individual Clan Deities of Bhotias	
		Clan	Deity
1.	Saai*	Biljuwal	Purbyal
2.	Herdyal*	Tolia	Raga
3.	Ajendi*	Jangpangi	Manhafaila
4.	Kodgari	Burfal	-do-
5.	Garhdevi	Pangtey	Aner
6.	Laandey*	Dhapwal	Danu
7.	Narsingh	Khinchiyal	Shankh
8.	Kalika	Mertolia	Khodai
9.	Churmal		
10.	Bhumiyal		
11.	Kalai		
12.	Bharari		
13.	Thathiyal		
14.	Nanda Devi		

(*Exclusive Bhotia deity)

There are only few deities which are exclusively worshipped by the Bhotias, otherwise most of the deities are also worshiped by their neighbouring peoples who are predominantly Hindu. This gives ample testimony that the Johari Bhotias have become highly Hinduised due to the acculturative influence of the neighbouring Hindu people. The deities like Saai, Herdyal, Ajendi Laandey are exclusive deities of Bhotiyas whereas the other deities like Bharare, Nar Singh, Kalika, etc. are all of Hindu origin. However, the individual clan deities are entirely of animistic nature and worshiped exclusively by the Bhotias.

The worshipping of most of these Bhotia deities has been related to the Bhotias migratory life, which was, in turn, related with their trading economy. It was only in the villages of their summer settlements or Malla Johar where Bhotias of all class and villages used to gather. In the Intermediate and winter settlements Bhotias of one particular village and clan used to get dispersed in different villages. Due to this congregation and dispersion of the Bhotia people of one place and different place, they had decided in propitiate most of their common and individual clans deities in the villages of their summer settlement. In was also otherwise important because it was here from where the Bhotias used to go to Tibet for effecting trade transactions. It was, again, in these villages' where Bhotias have had the temples of their common and individual clan deities like Nanda Devi, Raga, Shankh, Manhfoila, etc. The 'Purbayal devta' of Biljuwal clan is said to have its origin near a place called Dhilam which is situated near the village Lillam. Lillam village falls on the route leading to the summer settlement villages. That is why during the uphill migration, all Bhotias used to offer worship to this deity. The temple of some of the deities like Bharari, Kalika, Garhdevi Kodgarey etc. are located in the villages of winter settlements. Thus it is seen that the temples of the deities were located in the different villages of their three settlements. The migratory life of the Bhotias was so designed that during their uphill and downhill migrations, in connection with the trade, they were able to frequent these temples and offer the appropriate propitiation and worship. Since the worship of these deities involved the entire Bhotias of different villages, it reflected a sense of brotherhood, commonness, and enthusiasm. But after the cessation of the Bhotias trade, the migratory life was stopped which in turn, has affected the course of Bhotias religious observances and body of the religious beliefs.

RELIGIOUS FESTIVALS AND FAIRS

Johari Bhotias celebrate certain religious festivals and fairs. The festivals like *Saubali Ghiyutyohar* and *Bhoot-pitra-chechet* are celebrated at different occasions and have differential significance. 'Saubali' festival is celebrated at the end of September, to mark the end of the *Sawan Ka Mahina* which is considered to be in-auspicious by the Bhotias. Similarly '*Ghiyu-tyohar*' is celebrated to mark the initiation of the 'Bhado, month which is an auspicious month. '*Bhoot-Pitra-chechet*' festival is concerned with the ancestor worship. It is a matter of sheer coincidence that all these three festivals of the Johari Bhotias were being observed and celebrated in the villages of their summer settlements. And, after the cessation of their Tibetan trade, these religious festivals have lost their significance.

The religious fairs of the Bhotias are also their trade fairs. The important religious fairs of Bhotias are held at Bangeshwar Jauljibi, and Thal. These fairs generally centre round some local shrine, which earns a large income at the annual festival. The religious ritual of the fair consists of a dip in the river, if the fair is held on the banks of a river, or the worship of the presiding deity, if it centres round a shrine. Most of these fairs serve as the trade marts. Pant says, "the most numerous of these periodical marts are the annual fairs or *melas*. Apart from the commercial importance they have a religious and traditional aspect, and are not without their lighter side".

The religious-cum-trade fair of the Bhotias are observed in the following ways.

BAGESHWAR FAIR

Bageshwar lies 27 miles north of Almora, at an elevation of 3,143 feet. The annual fair is held here at the confluence of the river Sarju and Gomti on *Makar Shankranti* day, which falls roughly in the middle of January. Some 20,000 people, consisting mainly of Bhotias and Kumaonis assemble here. It is important both for the traders from north and the customers from the south. The fair begins one day before *Shankranti* (the first day of the solar month) and lasts for four or five days. In this fair, all kind of domestic animals, implements, articles of clothing, and indeed everything that is produced in the country, are displayed for sale. The Bhotia traders flock here in large numbers to act as middlemen or purchasers. Wool and woollen goods such as blankets, shawls and carpets form the chief merchandise of Bhotias. They also sell ponies, goats, and sheep. In addition to these, the Bhotias also sale yak-tails. Various kinds of skin and furs, muskpods, bear's gall, wooden bowls, borax, and leather skin bags of various shapes and sizes.

The ritualistic part of this religious fair consists in bathing before daybreak at the confluence (sangam)—the holy of holies whre the two reivers meet. After bathing an offering of water to the God Shiva in the Bagnath temple is essential. Those who are more religiously disposed continue this practice of bathing and offering water for three days in succession. This is known as *Trimaghi*, or the observances performed during the first three days of the month Magh (January-February). Among the men some shave their heads and offer rice balls to their departed ancestors.

JAULJIBI FAIR

Like '*Bageshwar*' *fair*, *Jauljibi* '*fair*' is also a religious-cum-trade fair. Jauljibi is situated some 6 miles north of Askot on the Nepal frontier, and on the confluence of the two rushing rivers. Beyond the Kali river the land belongs to the State of Nepal, and on the Indian side to the Pargana of Askote. The fair is held on the first day of the ninth Hindu month (mangsir), roughly corresponding with the middle of November This fair was started in the year 1914.

Jauljibi, besides lying at the confluence of Kali and Gori river also lies at the junction of four important routes viz. those leading from Nepal, Askote, Johar and Darma respectively. Hence, among the people assembled, Bhotias from *Parganas* Johar and Darma, Tibetans from Taklakat (until 1959), and Nepalese from Dote predominate. In this trade fair, ponies imported from Tibet by Bhotias formed the chief merchandise. Next to ponies, woollen goods of Tibet and of Bhotias have been the most important merchandise. These things could be had from this fair in the most genuine form, as Jauljibi is the first-trade mart visited by the Bhotias when they migrated Southwards from Tibet. Until recently some 15,000 people used to assemble here, and goods worth about two lacs were exchanged. From the commercial point of view it has been nearly as important as Bageshwar.

Jauljibi, unlike Bageshwar, did not possess any special religious significance. Bageshwar's greatness is attributed to its age-long tradition as being a place of pilgrimage. But some religious significance has also been attached to this place-'Jauljibi'—by constructing a temple on the junction of the two rivers. The people participating in this fair take a dip in the river and then offer worship in the temple.

In the interval between these two fairs the Bhotias used to make a few journeys to the Bhabar or terai marts, where they used to sell a considerable quantity of their goods. While raw wool was sold, the cereals, gur, and salt were purchased at Ramanagar and Haldwani. By the beginning of January, when the great fair at Bageshwar was held, the Bhotias, having completed their first trip to sub-montane marts, used to return to Bageshwar. After attending the fair the second trip to the Bhabar was undertaken, and was completed some time in April, when preparations for the march to Tibet was made.

THAL FAIR

In order to facilitate the preparations the third and the last fair of the Bhotia series is held at Thal which is known as Thal fair. Thal lies on the bank of the eastern Ramganga river. Here, fair is held in the middle of April and lasts for a week. In this fair all the Bhotias of the three passes i.e, Untadhura, Darma, and Byans, used to make journey through this place, as it is the meeting place of four important routes from Pithoragarh, Bageshwar, Askot and Tejam respectively. There, during the full week of the fair, a sort of "*clearance sale*" used to take place. The Bhotias used to try to sell all their unsold goods for the Bhabars at any price they could get; and the season's accounts between the hill or pahari peasants and the Bhotias were then settled. Some 12000 persons used to assemble here annually.

In this way it is seen that the religious fairs of the Bhotias have been closely related and attuned their trading activities. But now i.e., after the stoppage of the Bhotias' trading life, there has been significant change and decline in the nature and form of these Bhotia religious fairs. However, it remains to be examined in the next chapter.

5

Momentum of Change and Adaptation

Dynamism is one of the chief characteristics of culture. In the absence of dynamism, culture will be stagnated and it will put last nail in the coffin of a culture. Culture, which is a complex whole, is always in the process of making and remaking itself. The social, ecological and biological factors, technological developments, and cultural ingredients are continuously in operation on a particular, cultural working sometimes slowly, almost imperceptibly, and at times vigorously, almost revolutionising the traditional and patterned mode of life. The velocity of all these forces, playing from within and without are variant, so much so that the resultant forces pass through a line altogether different from those producing it, sometimes accelerating and sometimes retarding a particular force which determine the entire course of a socio-cultural life. All living cultures have stood the test of time because of their high adaptability and capacity to cope with such forces. In fact, every culture can be conceptualized as a strategy of adaptation, and each represents a unique social design. Change and adaptation in cultural system go together. If change is the niche of a culture, thus adaptation is its profession.

Bhotia society is the embodiment of such situation. A situation which reflects the dynamics of change and adaptive strategies in its socio-cultural system. Bhotia society has been undergoing change in its different elements for a long time. A close and minute study of the Bhotia society reveals that two distinct factors have been responsible for changes in its socio-cultural system. They are:

(1) *Changes Due to Contact Economics*

(2) *Changes Due to Economic Transformation*

The change which has been taking place in the Bhotia society due to their contact economics is rather slow, peripheral, and imperceptible and is manifest in their beliefs, values, and acculturated behaviour. But the change which has taken place in the Bhotia Society due to the transformation in the economic system is quite recent, organisational, institutional and radical. Though these two varieties of change are quite distinct and discernible, at times they cut across each other. In the present context, however, only the latter type of change i.e. change due to economic transformation, will be discussed for it concerns with the main theme of this study. Besides discussing the change, the present chapter also seeks to explain the adaptive processes which Bhotias have displayed to cope with the change in their economy and its correlated systems.

In the previous two chapters, it has been noted that Indo-Tibetan trade of the Bhotias has been the main pillar of their economic system and the other elements of economic and social systems have been an adjunct to it. The Bhotias have been carrying out trade with Tibet for last several centuries. But external factors, especially political developments, have always been important cause for bringing about changes in the patterned system of a society. Bhotia society too has experienced a radical change in their socio-cultural system due to the influence of powerful extraneous factors which were mainly political, and entirely beyond the control of Bhotia people. Due to the interference of the external forces the Bhotias had to lose their age-old trade relations with Tibet. Until the occupation of Tibet by Chinese forces in 1959, the Bhotias have had rather a smooth going trade relations with Tibet. But, with the change in the political set-up in Tibet, the Bhotias found themselves faced with the serious problem of losing their age-old occupation. The Chinese began interfering in their traditional trade with the Tibetans. Despite the Sino-Indian agreement of 1954, the Bhotias' trade situation worsened and in 1962, with the Chinese attack on India, it was completely stopped. The termination of Bhotias' traditional contacts with Tibet, has had profound effects on their entire way of life. The process of change in the Bhotia society, initially set in motion by the Chinese interference, has also been accelerated by the region's administrative organization. The economic development now taking place in the Bhotia Society cannot be divorced from the current changes in social attitudes and it would reveal that how economic, social, and political trends interlock and reinforce each other. The sudden disruption of the Indo-Tibetan trade, which was the main stay of Bhotias' economy and an adjunct to their socio-cultural system, has forced Bhotias to reorientate their economy and modify the socio-cultural life in conformity with the changed environment. In the discussion which follows it will be seen that how after 1962 i.e., after the cessation of Bhotia' trade, there has been almost a complete reorientation of the Bhotias' economy, and also, how they have adjusted their socio-cultural life to this change. While discussing the change and adaptive processes in the Bhotia society, attempts will be made to discuss the new socio-economic order with respect to the old order, and the problem of rehabilitation.

In order to understand the impact of the economic transformation on the Bhotias' socio-cultural life, it would be quite appropriate to examine it in the light of the following two broad aspects:

(i) Change in the Economic Organisation, and

(ii) Change in the Socio-cultural Elements.

CHANGE IN THE ECONOMIC ORGANISATION

The sudden disruption of the Bhotias' age-old trade relations with Tibet has had profound effect on their entire economic system. It has been noted that their economy has been an agglomeration of many elements such as, Indo-Tibetan trade, Agriculture, Pastoralism, and woollen industry. Of all these elements, the Indo-Tibetan trade of the Bhotias has been the principal element of their economy, while the other elements were dependent upon it. Therefore, it is quite natural to expect that when the main pillar of economy has been shattered, then there must have been considerable influence on its auxillary elements. And, in fact, the field study shows that the situation is in conformity to such an expectation. While the auxiliary elements of Bhotias' economy have undergone profound reorientation and assumed new dimension, the trade economy has been replaced by the commercial economy based on local conditions and resoufces.

AGRICULTURE

After losing trade as their principal occupation, Bhotias thought of falling back on agriculture. But, to their dismay, they could not adopt agriculture as the main element of their economy due to a variety of reasons. Prior to the cessation of their trans-Himalayan trade the Bhotias were practising agriculture only as their subsidiary occupation. Due to lack of agricultural know-how, poor physical conditions, and also due to the busy trade-schedules, Bhotias could not become the cultivator of their lnad holdings. They gave their land holdings to the local peasants for exploiting it on share-crop basis. Thus the local peasants became the tenant-cultivator of Bhotias and Bhotias developed a tenant-owner relationship with them. But this type of land tenureship due to the peculiar land exploitative pattern of Bhotias, which had got its root in the trade cycle, had a devastating effect on their possession of land holdings. Though the Zamindari Abolition Act was already introduced in 1952, it had its implication in the regions of Kumaon Himalayas only after its enactment in the year 1960.

The implementation of the enacted Zamindari Abolition Act gave a serious jolt to the land holdings Bhotias. It has been noted earlier that the Bhotias were only the Hissedars (owner) of their lands and not the owner cultivators. The local peasants comprising caste groups like Rajput, Brahman, Jethora, were the 'Sirtan' (tenant cultivators) of Bhotias. Hence, the enforcement of the Z.A. Act, without fixing any celling deprived most of the Bhotias of their land holdings. The tenant cultivator became the land owner and the owner of the land, but not the cultivator, became almost landless. Bhotias lost, except the land of their summer settlement, a considerable part of the land holdings of their intermediate and winter settlements. The land holdings of the summer settlements of Bhotias remained unaffected from the Z.A. Act because it was being exploited by the Shilpkars, Kunkiyas and Bhotias themselves. But, the land holdings of the summer seettlement did not prove of any great use because it was completely abandoned by the Bhotias after the closure of the trade.

From the following three tables an idea of the land holding pattern of the six Bhotia villages, in retrospect and prospect, can be seen. It is evident form the Table 8 that there has been considerable change in land holding size of the Bhotias. Barring the Dhapa village, the land holders of the other five villages have had to lose a major portion of their lands. The Bhotias of Dhapa village did not lose much land because, unlike the other Bhotias, they were primarily dependant on agriculture for their subsistence and only a few rich Bhotias were involved in trade. The Table 9 shows the transfer of Bhotias' lands in the Bhotia villages. It is quite clear from these tables that before the cessation of the Indo-Tibetan trade and enforcement of the Z.A. Act, Bhotias were having quite a substantive size of land holding. But now they are hardly having enough land to subsist primarily on it. Besides the small size of land holdings, the other factors which restricted Bhotias from falling back on agriculture is the arid nature of the soil. In a study of 224 Bhotia families of different villages it was found that only 2.42% Bhotia families are practising agriculture as their primary occupation, whereas 2º.46% Bhotia families are practising it as only their subsidiary occupations. 45.08% Bhotia families have practically no agricultural base in their subsistence strategies. These families have completely shunned agriculture and depend on commercial sources available to them in their regions. The changes which have occurred in agricultural activities of the Bhotias due to their heavy dependence on trade and due to the enforcement of the Z.A. Act, 1961, are of following nature:

i) for some Bhotia families, agriculture became the primary occupation while for some it continues to form an important subsidiary occupations.
ii) Some Bhotia families have completely left agriculture.
iii) Some families became landless, while others lost a considerable part of their land holding.
iv) Bhotia families learnt the value of land ownership and now they practise settled cultivation.

PASTORALISM

Prior to the cessation of the Bhotias trade with Tibet the cattle of Bhotias, which consisted of sheep, goat, mule, ponies, jibu, etc., formed one of the important elements of Bhotias' economy. It served the following purposes :

TABLE—8

Pattern of l and Transfer and Change in the Land Holding Size Among the Bhotias

Sl. No.	Village	Land Holders and Land Holdings before 1961*			Land Holders Land Holdings after 1961*			Difference (before & after 1961)	
		Total Land Hol-ders	Total Land Holdings (in Nali)	Average Land Hol-dings Size	Total Land Hol-ders	Total Land Holdings	Average Land Hol-ding Size	In the No. of Land Holders	In the Size of Land Holdings (in Nali)
1.	Jallath	102	1166	11.43	137	804	5.87	35 (+)	362
2.	Malla	25	1435	57.40	32	1118	34.94	7 (+)	317
3.	Suring	137	1367	9.98	125	1060	8.48	12 (—)	307
4.	Talla	39	583	14.95	98	271	2.77	59 (+)	292
5.	Dummer Malla	60	785	13.08	62	491	7.92	2 (+)	294
6.	Dummer Dhapa	48	2445	50.94	82	1709	20.84	34 (+)	736
7.	Darkot	117	927	7.92	109	776	7.12	8 (—)	151

Note : 240 square yards is equal to 1 Nali and 20 Nalis of land make one acre.

TABLE—9

Transfer of Bhotia Lands

Sl. No.	Bhotia Villages	Total Land Holders	Total holding.	Number & Percentage of Holders who Lost: No. Land	Less than 20 Nali	21 to 40 Nali	40 to 60 Nali	61 to 80 Nali	80 to 100 Nali	101 Nali and above.
1.	Jallath	102	30 (29.41%)	32 (31.37%)	33 (32.35%)	5 (4.90%)	2 (1.96%)	—	—	
2.	Malla Ghorpatta	25	12 (48.0%)	—	9 (36.0%)	1 (4.%)	2 (8.%)	1 (4.%)	—	—
3.	Suring	137	94 (68.61%)	—	32 (23.36%)	6 (4.38%)	3 (2.19%)	—	—	2 (1.46%)
4.	Talla Dummer	39	7 (17.95%)	15 (38.46%)	10 (25.64%)	5 (12.82%)	2 (5.13%)	—	—	—
5.	Malla Dummer	60	39 (65.00%)	—	16 (26.67%)	4 (6.67%)	1 (1.67%)	—	—	—
6.	Dhapa	48	—	28 (58.33%)	15 (31.25%)	1 (2.08%)	--	1 (2.08%)		3 (6.25%
7.	Darkot	117	66 (56.41%)	16 (13.67%)	31 (26.41%)	1 (85%)	2 (1.70%)	–	—	—
		528	248 (45.08%)	146 (29.02%)	22 (4.37%)	11 (2.18%)	(.39%)	2 (.39%)		5 (.99%)

i) transportation of the items of export and import.
ii) coarse wool for the woollen industry.
iii) provided with hides and skin and mutton.
iv) beasts of burden for transporting the commodities of pahari people.

But, after the closure of the Bhotia's trade, there has been a fundamental change in the pastoral life of the Bhotia. The most important change is manifest in the functional use of the cattle as beasts of burden. Due to the stoppage of the trade, Bhotias no more required their animals for the transportation of export and import items. Further, due to the introduction of the wheeled transport in the hill and border regions of the Bhotia region, the cattle of the Bhotias lost their role in transporting the different items in the uphill and downhill villages. All this had a tremendous effect on the size of the Bhotias' cattle wealth. Most Bhotia families either sold out their pack animals or consumed them for mutton purposes. In the present time, Bhotias have become deprived of their animals. In the study of Bhotia families, it was found that out of 224 families, only 21 families (10.6%) are having cattle. The number of sheep and goats has reached to a deplorably low. The decline in the number of sheep has greatly affected the Bhotias' woollen industry. During their trading years, Bhotias were obtaining a fair amount of wool from their own sheep. But now-a-days only 11.1% Bhotia families are dependent on the wool from their own sheep. The other Bhotia families are procuring wool from the government organisation and some co-operative societies. The families who are still retaining some sheep, goats, and ponies use them primarily as pack-animals. They supply the food-grains, and other items to the para-military troops stationed in the border regions where no motor vehicles ply. For the transportation of various items Bhotia families rely more on ponies and mules than on sheep and goat. During the trade economy, almost each Bhotia trader owned at least 150-300 sheep and goats, 10-15 mules and ponies, 5-10 jibus, etc. But now-a-days these animals have become more or less extinct from most of the Bhotia villages. In the present study of the 16 Bhotia villages only in five Bhotia villages some families were discovered with having sheep, goats, mules and ponies. But even with them, the number of these pack-animals was very low. Out of 21 Bhotia families who owned cattle, only four families owned sheep and goats between 100 to 150, 8 families between 50 to 100, and 11 families had less than 50 sheep and goats. The number of mules and ponies did not exceed more than four.

The sharp decline in the size of the pack animals of Bhotias can also be attributed, besides the fall in the value of these animals for transportation purposes, to the shortage of pasture lands. Bhotias stopped their uphill and downhill migration after the cessation of their trade with Tibet. The migratory life of the Bhotias was so designed and regulated that their pack-animals like sheep, goats, mules, etc. used to get sufficient pasture land in the alpine and terai regions. But after the cessation of the nomadic habits it became a difficult task for the Bhotias to graze their animals in the limited and meagre pasture lands available to them in the surrounding regions of their settled villages. That is why after the cessation of the trade with Tibet, most of the Bhotia families preferred to pursue other occupations from the money obtained from selling their pack-animals or beasts of burden. Thus, this change in the Bhotias' pastoral economy, due to the cessation of their trade with Tibet, marked a shift from pastoral economy to commercial economy based on local sources and conditions.

WOOLLEN INDUSTRY

Woollen Industry of Bhotias has not only been a means of earning livelihood but also gave a picture of their rich craftsmanship. Until the closure of the trade, both these two points were intimately linked with the Bhotia's socio-economic life. But after the closure of the trade, the Bhotias' woollen industry has witnessed a great set-back. The most important factor is the acute shortage of raw-wool. In the trading operations of the Bhotias, the import of raw wool from Tibet formed a major objective. While the imported raw wool was sold out by Bhotias, a good account of wool was retained for use in the making of woollen clothes. But with the stoppage of the trade, the import of raw wool from Tibet was also automatically stopped. The non-availability of Tibetan wool, and the gradual decline in the number of Bhotias' sheep population have had tremendous effect on the successful running of and earning from the woollen industry of Bhotias. Secondly, the government policy even restricted Bhotias from purchasing raw wool from Nepal and other sources. All this had almost left the Bhotias' woollen industry on the verge of its closure. But, in the meantime Govt. smelt the need of the situation and did some commendable job which helped Bhotias in reviving their woollen industry. The Bhotias of Johar Valley felt greatly relieved when for the first time a "Khadi and Gramodyog Commission" was opened in Johar Valley in the year 1965. The acute shortage of raw wool for the Bhotias' woollen industry was fulfilled by the Khadi Gram odyog Commission. The Commission started giving raw wool and spinning and weaving implements to Bhotias at concessional rates. The spinning and weaving implements which are being made available to the Bhotias can be seen from the following Table (10)

TABLE—10

Table showing the Implements which Bhotia Obtain from Khadi odyog Gram Commission

Sl. no.	Implements	Original Cost	Subsidised Rate for the Bhotia
1.	Loom	Rs. 300/-	Rs. 125/-
2.	Charkha	Rs. 50/-	Rs. 12.50/-
3.	Carding Brush	Rs. 7/-	Rs. 2.50/-
4.	Wire-heeled (100 pieces)	Rs. 15/-	Rs. 5.00/-
5.	Reel	Rs. 15/-	Rs. 5.00/-
6.	Takli (spindle)	Paise 40	Paise 10

Though the implements did not prove of much use because most of the Bhotias already possessed. But, these new implements definitely helped them in raising the work efficiency. Again, it is seen that though the Kh. Gr. Commission is providing wool to Bhotias, this scheme has hardly been able to provide them a viable income from the woollen industry. As a matte of fact the Kh. Gr. Comm. is acting as a supplier of the wool and also as the consumer of the finished product. The role of Bhotias is only to act as craftsman. They receive raw wool from the Commission to manufacture different varieties of woollen materials. After manufacturing the woollen garments, rugs, carpets, etc. Bhotias return these materials to the Commission, and in return they obtain their labour cost. All this is done in a very strict manner by the Commission. They give wool to the Bhotias by weighing it and then receive the finished products in terms of its weight and quality. From the Table 11, an idea about the Bhotias' dealings with the Kh. Gr. Commission can be developed.

TABLE—11

Bhotias' Dealing with Khadi Gram odyog Commission

Sl. no.	Woollen Material	Raw wool required	Labour charges for the item	Time consumed
1.	Dann (Carpet)	8 Kg.	Rs. 100/-	One month
2.	Thulma (blanket)	6.1/2 Kg.	Rs. 28/-	15 days
3.	Chutka (rug)	8 to 10 Kg.	Rs. 40/-	One month
4.	Pankhi (wrapper)	1 Kg. woollen yarn	Rs. 5/-	3 in a day
5.	Shawl	500 gm -do-	Rs. 5/-	-do-
6.	Mafflar	200 gm -do-	Rs. 1.50	5 to 6 in a day
7.	Trid	200 gm woollen per metre	Rs. 1/- to 4/-	3 metre in a day
8.	Sweter	400 gm -do-	Rs. 4/- for half & 7 for full	5 days
9.	Caps	50 gm -do-	Rs. 1/-	2 caps a day

The price of the different woollen products which Bhotias manufacture out of the raw wool given to them by the Khadi Gr. Commission, keep varying according to the quality of the finished product. It is generally calculated by counting the humber of knots and seeing the smoothness of the woollen products. For carpet weaving, the price is fixed on the basis of the numbrr of knots employed therein. The Khadi Gr. Commission pays 70 paise per knot for the carpet of a typical Bhotia design, whereas Re. 1/-is paid for the carpet of Persian design.

The Khadi Gr. Commission has definitely been able to keep the Bhotias' woollen industry alive, but it has not been able to encourage spinning and weaving activities. This is due to the fact that Bhotias are not getting proper price of their skill and labour. The Khadi Gr. Commission is giving them only a fraction of their labour in terms of money. For making a carpet, a Bhotia man and woman has too spend a month in spinning and weaving. And for this labour, they get only Rs. 100/- which hardly amounts to Rs. 3.25 a day.

The Khadi Gr. Commission has differential significance for the different sections of the Bhotias. The Bhotias who are economically poor and cannot afford to buy raw wool from the open market and also wait for until the marketing of their woollen products, have shoown almost absolute dependance on the Khadi Gr. Commission. This is so because the Khadi Gr. Commission not only helps them in procuring wool but also provides them market for their woollen materials by readily purchasing their products. And this way such Bhotia families have lost their autonomy and monopoly over the woollen industry. Some rich Bhotia families, however, are still enjoying prosperity in their woollen industry. They purchase raw wool from the Khadi Gr. Commission and other sources and prepare different woollen materials to which they sell out in the open market. Such Bhotia families are earning good profit from their woollen industry because they are getting handsome price for their woollen materials. But the number of such Bhotia families is extremely few. Some Bhotia families have even started procuring loan from the State Bank of India, Munsiari Branch. In the present survey it was found that 150 Bhotias have taken a loan of Rs. 75,000/- at the concessional rate of 4% interest for purchasing wool.

Besides the Khadi Gr. Commission, there is one more Government Organisation which is engaged in reviving and developing the Bhotias' woollen industry. This organisation mainly imparts training to the Bhotia weavers and the other people of the Bhotia region. For the first time a carpet weaving centre was opwened by the U.P. Government in the Bhotia village 'Milankutia' in the year 1967. This training centre ran from 1967 to 1977 and was known was 'Shawl Evam Galicha Kendra'. Besides imparting training in weaving techniques, this organisation was also concerned with the consumption of the finished woollen materials of the Bhotias. But this organisation was finally closed in the year 1977 due to financial stringencies. Again, in the year 1977, on 28th March the U.P. Government opened a new carpet training centre in Munsiari which is known as 'Galicha Prashikchan Kendra'. This organisation imparts training only to the women students and pays a stipend of Rs. 60/- to each trainee students of age group between 16 to 35 years. During the survey it was found that 45 trainee students were enrolled in this carpet weaving centre. Of the 45 trainee students, only 10 trainees belonged to the Bhotia community, whereas there were 25 scheduled castes, and 10 trainees of other castes like Rajput and Brahman.

Thus, due to the stoppage of the trade, there has been tremendous effect on the structure and organisation of Bhotia's woollen industry. In the present times, most of the Bhotias have lost their autonomy and monopoly over the woollen industry which they enjoyed prior to the cessation of their Indo-Tibetan trade.

TRADE WITH THE PAHARI PEOPLES

Besides having trade relations with the Tibetans, Bhotias were also having prosperous trade relations with the local 'pahari' peoples. While trade with the Tibetans was carried out in the summer, trade with the 'pahari' people was effected in the winter i.e., after Bhotias' migration to the lower valleys from their summer settlement. In the trade with the local 'pahari' people, the items as were brought from Tibet and the woollen products of the Bhotias, formed the principal objects of transactions. It is, therefore, obvious that the Bhotias' trade with the 'pahari' peoples was closely related with their Tibetan trade. And with the cessation of the Tibetan trade, the Bhotias' trade with the 'pahari' people has also almost come to an end. Now a days the Bhotias are hardly anything, except other than their own woollen materials and the grocery items of the Indian markets, to sell to the 'pahari' people. In the absence of the Tibetan trade and the trade with the 'pahari' people, the Bhotias have now sought dependance on a commercial economy which is largely being catered in the backdrop of the local and indigenous sources. This trend has led to many a Bhotia families to settle down with permanent shops in the urban and semi-urban centres of the lesser Himalayan regions. But the nature of this trade, which the Bhotias have started doing with the Kumaoni (pahari) people, has considerably changed. While in the pre-1962 period the Bhotias' trade with the local 'pahari' people was based more or less on purely barter terms, in the present times, it is strictly a cash dealing.

EMERGENT ECONOMIC TRENDS

It is no doubt true that the stoppage of the Indo-Tibetan trade has forced the Bhotias to reorientate their economic elements like agriculture, pastoralism, woollen industry, etc. But in the present times, these elements of Bhotias' economy do not represent the sole means of the livelihood of Bhotias. Due to the change in the economic set-up and the gradual expansion of the Government's interference in the development of the Bhotia region, Bhotias have sought dependance on a variety of occupations which are largely based on the local sources and conditions. The main elements of the Bhotias' economy, which have emerged in the last one and a half decade, can be discussed under the rubric of the following occupations.

SHOP KEEPING

After the closure of the trade Bhotias, for a long time, faced difficulty in finding an alternate occupation for them. But it is quite true to say that the man's socio-economic life is modified in adaptation to the demands and potentials inherent in his cultural equipments and related techniques. Bhotias, too, have displayed such a modification in their economic organisation which is in conformity to their age-old economic system that was essentially based on trade and commerce. In the changed economic set-up, Bhotias preferred to fall back, besides their traditional occupations, on a trading economy nurtured in the configuration of local sources. Among the Bhotias, now shop keeping forms the major occupation. Some rich Bhotias who were having capital and cash money got settled at different places by opening shops of different commodities like, cloth, foodgrains, stationaries, hotels, etc. In this occupation, Bhotias were greatly facilitated by the merchants of the 'terai' regions. Bhotias were having good contacts with the traders, wholesellers and retailers, of the terai region during their trade with Tibet, and the merchants have had profound faith on the Bhotias. Such merchants came to the rescue of Bhotias by giving them different articles of sale on credit and part payment. This way the itinerant traders of trans Himalayan regions got converted into the settled traders. The occupation of shop-keeping started flourishing because the Bhotias had a good cultural base in the trade economy. But this occupation prompted many Bhotia families to abandon their home villages and get settled at places where the prospects for opening shops were bright. In the present survey of 224 Bhotia families, it was found that 80 families have migrated to the urban and semi-urban centres of lesser Himalayan regions like Thal, Bageshwar, Garur, Haldwani, Gwaldham, etc. for doing shop-keeping as a means of livelihood. Of the 80 families living in the urban and semi-urban settings, 51 families (63.75%) are doing shop-keeping as their primary occupation and only 1 Bhotia family is doing it as his subsidiary occupation (table–13). This incidence of shop-keeping, however, is quite low among those Bhotia families who are living in their original village and geographic setting. Only 14% and 12.73% Bhotia families of winter and intermediate settlements do shop-keeping as their primary occupation (Table 13).

GOVERNMENT SERVICE

There was a time, especially before the cessation of the trade, when doing Government service was considered as a derogatroy work and a sort of slavery by the Bhotias. They were seldom interested in going for Govt. services. It is no doubt true that about two decades back there was a great dearth of literate and educated persons among the Bhotias who could be absorbed in the Govt. services. But even during those days the educated persons abstained from doing Govt. services. However, in recent times this tendency of the Bhotias towards Govt. services, has changed considerably. Now, after the closure of the Bhotias' trade, Government services have become a potential source for earning a livelihood by the Bhotias. Subsequent to the cessation of the trade with Tibet, Bhotias are increasingly being absorbed in Government and semi-Govt., and private concerns. This trend got further momentum after the declaration of Bhotias as the scheduled tribe in the year 1967. Bhotias, after attaining the status and category of scheduled tribe, started getting reservations in Govt. services. and in admission to the educational institutions Now a days, Bhotias both males and females, are working in different Govt. departments. They enjoy different positions in these services. Besides a number of white collar jobs, many Bhotias are working as teachers, clerks and peons, etc. A number of military and para-military units established in the Bhotia regions also provide opportunities for earning a regular cash income to the Bhotias. The Bhotias who are engaged in Government services have greately helped in the maintainance of their family members. Those posted out-station remit a regular help to their parents both in cash and kind. This has led to quite a good number of Bhotia families to depend on the money-order economy. In the present survey of 224 Bhotia families, who are living in a different eco-cultural settings, it was found that 15.8% families are doing Government services as their main occupation, whereas about 8.48% families have been doing it as their subsidiary occupation. (Table 12).

CONTRACT TAKING

Some Bhotia families have also resorted to the occupation of contract taking. The most important contracts which Bhotias take relate to road construction, soil cutting, house construction, ration supply to the military units, and supply of medicinal herbs to the private and Govt. agencies dealing with the manufacture of aurvedic medicines. The contract work. is done mainly by those Bhotia families who are economically sound and can afford to risk their money in the contract works This occupation of Bhotias was on the peak when, after the Sino-Indian border conflicts, the border roads were being made motorable. Contracts for this work mainly went to Bhotias because they were not only wealthy people of the region but also enterprising. Now a days, contract taking has assumed one of the important elements in the subsistence strategies of Bhotias which are largely based on local sources. In the present study of 224 Bhotia families it was found that 8 and 6 families (3.57% and 2.68%) are doing the occupation of contract taking as their main and subsidiary occupations respectively (table-12).

CASUAL LABOUR

Some Bhotia families who are economically poor and

downtrodden, have started working as casual labourers in the surrounding areas and villages. It is really pathetic to see Bhotias working as casual labourers, because only few decades back they were prosperous traders and had a viable economic situation. However, the occupation of casual labourer is done mainly by the Kunkiya Bhotias because they are mostly landless people and lack sufficient capital to invest in some prestigious occupations. The Bhotias who work as casual labourers are engaged mainly in the jobs pertaining to road construction, soil cutting, herb collection, etc. Casual labour as an occupation is done mostly by the Bhotias of winter settlement and not by those Bhotias who are settled in the intermediate and semi-urban and urban settlements. This is so because Bhotias of these settlements are either engaged in shop-keeping or agriculture as their main occupations which in contrary to the Bhotias of the winter settlement. The percentage of Bhotia families who are dependant on casual labour can be seen from the table-12.

LIQUOR VENDING

Prior to the cessation of the trade, the Johari Bhotias used to manufacture alcoholic drinks like 'Chakti' and 'Jaan' mainly for individual and social purposes. But after the cessation of the trade, the Bhotias have started manufacturing alcohol for commercial purposes. But, again, it is seen that this sort of occupation is restricted mainly among the Bhotias of Intermediate settlement. This is so because the 'tehsil' headquarter is situated in this settlement and many people visit here for different sort of work. During their brief sojourn over there, they visit Bhotia villages for obtaining alcoholic drinks. This has led to many Bhotias families to depend on the income derived from liquor vending. In the present survey it was found that out of 110 Bhotia families of intermediate settlement, 3 families (2.73%) have taken up liquor vending as their main source of occupation and 56 families (51.91%) are doing it as their subsidiary occupations (table-12).

From the foregoing discussion it is clear that after the stoppage of the Bhotias' trade with Tibet, there has been more or less complete reorientation and emergence of new subsistence strategies in the economic structure of the Bhotias. A complete picture of the subsistence stratagies of Bhotias, which are based on the configuration of different main and subsidiary occupations, can be seen from the table-12 and table-13. It is quite clear from these tables that the economic structure of the Bhotias have now a stratified and disjointed orientation in comparison to the pre-1962 period when the Bhotias economy was centred round the one principal occupation i.e., the Tibetan trade. Subsequent to the cessation of the trade, the different occupations of Bhotias have differential significance for the Bhotias inhabiting the different eco-cultural settings.

TABLE—12

Occupational Categories of Bhotias

Sl. No.	Occupational Categories	Nature of Occupation Main No.	Percentage	Subsidiary No.	Percentage
(1)	(2)	(3)	(4)	(5)	(6)
1.	Agriculture	48	21.42%	66	29.46%
2.	Wool work	44	19.64%	70	31.25%
3.	Service	34	15.18%	19	8.48%
4.	Sheep Rearing	15	6.70%	9	4.02%
5.	Shop Keeping	70	31.25%	5	2.23%
6.	Contract Taking	8	3.57%	6	2.68%
7.	Casual Labour	4	1.79%	1	.45%
8.	Other	1	.45%	3	1.34%
		224	100.00%	179	79.91%

45 (20.09%) families have no subsidiary occupation.

TABLE—13

Settlement Pattern & Occupational Variability of Bhotias

Sl. No.	Settlement Site	Total No. of families	Nature of occupation	OCCUPATIONS Agriculture	Wool work	Service	OF Sheep Rearing	BHOTIAS Shop Keeping	Contract taking	Casual	Other
1.	Intermediate Settlement (Goriphat)	110	Main	28 25.45%	46 36.36%	16 14.55%	9 9.18%	14 12.73%	2 1.82%	4 3.64%	3 2.73%
			Subsidiary	49 44.55%	28 25.45%	16 14.55%	7 6.36%	1 .91%	2 1.82%	1 .91%	56 50.91%
2.	Winter Settlement (Talla Johar)	34	Main	16 47.06%	12 32.35%	6 15.65%	— —	5 14.71%	— —	— —	— —
			Subsidiary	10 29.41%	18 52.84%	2 5.88%	— —	3 8.82%	— —	— —	— —
3.	Urban & Semi-Urban Settings	80	Main	4 5.00%	4 5.00%	12 15.00%	2 2.5 %	51 63.75	6 7.5 %	— —	— —
			Subsidiary	7 8.75%	3 44.25%	1 1.25%	2 2. 5%	1 1.25%	4 5.00%	— —	— —
	Total 224										

(The village-wise distribution of the occupational categories of Bhotias can be seen in the Table No. 3 in Appendix V)

CHANGE IN THE SOCIO-CULTURAL ELEMENTS

The socio-cultural life of the Bhotia has been closely attuned to their trading economy. But, with the change in the trade-based economy and its associated elements, there has also been substantial change in the socio-cultural elements of the Bhotias. In discussing the socio-cultural elements of Bhotias that have been affected by their economic activity, I shall rely on the common distinctions between the *'evaluational'* and *'existential'* aspects of culture. Smelser (1965) says, "evaluational aspect of culture refers to that which is considered desirable in a system of cultural values ; that which ought to be pursued by members of a society. The existential aspect of culture, on the other hand, refers to assertions concerning what man, society, and nature are like. In relation to economic activities, these two aspects of culture raise two types of questions ;

(i) Do economic activities occupy a major place in the cultural value system ? Are they valued as an end in themselves, or viewed as sub-ordinated to the pursuit of a harmonious socio-cultural life ?

(ii) What is the nature of man ? Is he defined as being economically motivated or are these features of his existence underplayed ?"

After having establishmed answers to these questions in relation to the Bhotia society, one is better able to analyse the relation between values and ideologies on the one hand and economic activities on the other. It is quite imperative to make clear that the term 'ideology' quite often refers to the assertions about the nature of the persons in a social situation and their relations to one another. It also gives a broader meaning to activities that otherwise might not be immediately intelligible ; or more strongly, they may be used to induce people in a system of social relations that they should do things they might not otherwise wish to do.

In the previous chapter it has already been seen that how the economic activities of Bhotias forced them to adopt a peculiar way of socio-cultural life. But, due to the stoppage of the Indo-Tibetan trade and the resultant reorientation in the economic activities, there has also been considerable change in the elements of Bhotias' socio-cultural life. Thus by examining the existential aspect of culture in relation to old evaluational aspect of culture and its relation with the economic activities of Bhotias, current changes in the elements of Bhotias' socio-cultural life can be ascertained. Here, again, I shall consider the changes with respect to the old social order.

SETTLEMENT PATTERN

Prior to the cessation of the Indo-Tibetan trade, the Bhotias of Johar Valley were having three sets of proliferated dwellings in three settlements viz. Summer, Winter, and Intermediate Settlements. All these three settlements of Bhotias have had differential significance for them. While the summer settlement served as the storage for exportable items, the other two settlements provided them with foodgrains and vegetables because the lands of these two settlements are fit for two crops in a year. The summer settlement of Bhotia not only served as the centre for storage of export items but also as the centre from where Bhotias used to start their trans-Himalayan journey for trading with the Tibetans. But, after the stoppage of the Tibetan trade the summer settlement of the Johari Bhotias lost its importance as trade depot. And, since the lands of this region, due to physical conditions are not fit for profitable agriculture, the Johari Bhotias deserted their summer settlement and got settled in their other two settlements. However, the occupation of the villages of these two settlements has been done more or less in the old pattern i.e. clan based villages. Members of each Bhotia clan got dispersed in the villages of their winter and intermediate settlements. Thus, the stoppage of the trade with Tibet brought two fundamental changes in the settlement pattern of Bhotias :

(i) Abandonment of summer settlement, and

(ii) Sedentrization of itinerant Bhotia people.

Besides these two important features, the other significant change is reflected in the settlement of semi-urban and urban centres like Thal, Bageshwar, Garur, Didihat, Haldwani, etc., by some of the Johari Bhotia families. In the present survey of 80 such families, i.e. those who have permanently migrated to these semi-urban and urban centres, about 30% Bhotia families left their home villages and original socio-economic environment within five years after 1962. Whereas the other 70% of such families have occupied these centres in the last 10 to 15 years of time period. Even, now-a-days, such migrations are increasingly taking place. The principal occupation of most of these Bhotia families, afier 1962, has become shop-keeping (Table 12) which is different from the Bhotias of other two settlements. The Bhotias of intermediate and winter settlements are following a diverse type of occupation like agriculture. service (Govt.), shop-keeping, contract-taking etc.

SEMI-NOMADISM AND TRANSHUMANCE

Until 1962, the Bhotias' life style was characterized by a semi-nomadic and transhumant life. Their trading activities and cattle wealth, besides the climatic factor, necessitated them to make seasonal movements in the different set of fixed settlements, and in the alpine and terai pastures. But, after the disruption of their trading contacts with Tibetans, there has been remarkable change in the migratory activities of Bhotias. Bhotias not only ceased to migrate in their different set of settlements but also effected considerable contractions in their transhumant activities. It has been noted earlier that the Bhotias' transhumant activities have been a combination of greater and lesser transhumance. But the stoppage of the trade and the consequent decrease in the size of their flocks, the transhumant life of the Bhotias has been reduced to the lesser transhumance category. Now, with their very few number of flocks, mostly sheep and goats, Bhotias keep moving within the mountain regions from lower to higher slopes.

While most Bhotia families have abandoned their summer settlement and stopped the migratory life by settling down in the intermediate and winter settlements, there are some Bhotia families who still make periodic journeys to the villages of summer settlements. But the number of such families is extremely few, and they mostly belong to their present winter and intermediate settlement. There is hardly any family, from among those who are now-a-days settled in the semi-urban and urban centres, who makes uphill movement for going to the villages of summer settlement. In the present survey of 144 Bhotia families of intermediate and winter settlement (110 from intermediate and 34 from winter settlements respectively), 25 families (22.73 %) from intermediate and 5 families (14.71%) from winter settlement were still found making uphill journey for the villages of summer settlements. These families go to their original or parental villages with their families, plough animals and sheep and goats. In contrast to the pre-1962 period when the Johari Bhotias used to frequent their villages of summer settlement mainly for effecting trade transactions, these days some Bhotia families come over here for mainly agricultural purposes. Here, they grow potato, buck-wheat, and barley by staying for about three months. Since most part of the villages of summer settlements have been deserted by the Johari Bhotias, such families, who come over here for agricultural purposes, get enough virgin and unclaimed land for ploughing to obtain the cash crops like potato and buck wheat. It is quite evident from this tendency of these Bhotias families that either they do-not have land in their downhill villages or they have lost their land holdings after the implementation and enforcement of Zamindari Abolition Act, 1960 ; and have no other means for subsistence. In the absence of the sufficient number of pack animals and companion migrants of one and the same village, these families have to undertake a very strenuous uphill journey and lead a monotonous life over there. No special arrangements for these families, except with regard to the education of their children, have been made by Government to facilitate the migration of these people in the changed socio-economic conditions.

The recent changes in the settlement pattern, semi-nomadic and transhumant life of Johari Bhotias, however, are in sharp contrast to the changes which have occurred in the life style of other Bhotia groups like Shauka, Tolchha, Marchha, and Jaad Bhotias. Unlike the Johari Bhotias, the other Bhotia groups, despite the stoppage of their Indo-Tibetan trade, could not stop their semi-nomadic life and abandon the villages of summer settlement. Barring the Jaad Bhotias, who had to desert the villages of their summer settlements for border's security measures, all other Bhotia groups have continued their itinerant life and undertake seasonal movements in the villages of their summer and winter settlements. This is due to the fact that the summer settlements of these Bhotia groups i.e., Shauka, Tolchha, and Marchha, have served the dual purpose. These Bhotia groups not only maintained their trade depots in the villages of summer settlement, but also the cultivable lands. These Bhotia groups are having practically no land holdings for cultivation purposes, in the villages of their winter settlements. That is why, it is seen that these Bhotia groups, who have mostly transformed from a trade to agricultural economy, have persisted with their semi-nomadic life. During the summer they move to their summer villages, and with the start of snowfall in these regions, they again descend to the villages of their winter settlements. The Johari Bhotias, unlike these Bhotia groups, managed to stop their migratory life and to get settled because they were having three proliferated set of dwellings. Incidentally, also, the Johari Bhotias have had their cultivable lands in the villages of lower altitude settlements.

FAMILY AND HOUSEHOLD ORGANIZATION

It has been noted earlier that prior to the cessation of

Bhotias' trade with Tibet, the basis of their household organization, which was closely related to the trading activities of the Bhotias, was joint family. But, after the stoppage of the trade, their has been some noteworthy changes in the family and household organization of Bhotias with the reorientation of the economic activities which has been done on the basis of a diverse type of occupations, the Bhotia were also required to reorganise the form or made of their family and household organization.

In the present day economic set-up of Bhotias, the form of the Bhotia family has become predominantly nuclear, followed by joint and extended families, and also some single person households. The main reason for this change in the form of family can be attributed to the proliferation of the joint families into the villages of winter and summer settlements. During the trade economy joint families of Bhotias used to migrate collectively in the villages of different set of settlements. But due to the stoppage of the itinerant life and consequent disintegration of families of one clan into two villages i.e., one village from each settlement, the Bhotias were forced to break the ties of joint families into that of nuclear families. The other important reason is the diversification in the economic activities of the Bhotias. The trading activities of the Bhotias required a large number of persons and hence, the joint family was a must. But in the present configuration of the economic activities, Bhotias neither require the help of many persons, nor they can afford them in the kinship network of joint family. This has naturally developed a sense of individualism among Bhotias. But, it is seen, in spite of the aforesaid constraints, that the joint family, quite often supplemented by extended families, is not absent amongst the Johari Bhotias. In the present survey it was found that most of the joint families were formed of the old parents, daughter-in-law, unmarried grandchildren, and the married sons who are living outside the village either for doing govt. service or higher studies. In such joint families, the main source of income is derived from the earnings of the adult married males, which is supplemented by the earnings from the woollen handicrafts manufactured by the old parents and female members of the family.These joint families are sometimes joined by close relative, either for availing the educational facilities or for temporary subsistence, and thus give it a form of extended families. Single person household in the Bhotia village mostly consists of the male or female widows who are leading an independent life. Such persons get a fixed amount of money (Rs. 40/-) from the Government in the form of aid for the 'Nirashrit Widhwas' (indipendent widows). Since this amount of money is extremely meagre for subsistence, the close relatives or the rich persons of the village make casual help in the form of cash and kind to the independent widows.

The family type among the Bhotias can be seen from the Table 14. It is quite clear from the table that out of 224 Bhotia families, 143 (63.84%) are nuclear, 64 (28.57%) are joint, 14 (6.25%) are extended families and only 3 (1.34%) are single person households. This figure is indicative of the predominance of nuclear families in the Bhotia society. It can be again seen from the Table 15 that the incidence of nuclear families is more among those families who are settled in the urban and semi-urban centres than those settled in the winter and intermediate settlements.

TABLE—14

Family Type Among The Bhotias

Serial No.	Family Type	Number	Percentage
1.	Nuclear	143	63.84%
2.	Joint	64	28.57%
3.	Extended	14	6.25%
4.	Single Person Household	3	1.34%
	Total :	224	100.00

TABLE—15

Family Type in the Theer Bhotia Settlements

Sl. No.	Settlement	No. of Families	Family Type Nuclear	Joint	Extended	Single Person
1.	Intermediate	110	65 (50.09%)	37 (33.63%)	6 (5.45%)	2 (1.8 %)
2.	Winter	34	22 (64.70%)	7 (20.58%)	4 (11.76%)	1 (2.89%)
3.	Urban and Semi-urban	80	56 (70%)	20 (25%)	4 (5%)	---
	Total :	224	143 (63.85%)	64 (28.57%)	14 (6.25%)	3 (1.34%)

SOCIAL STRATIFICATION

Subsequent to the stoppage of the Indo-Tibetan trade, there has hardly been any change in the structure of the rank stratified society of the Bhotias. But, certain changes have definitely crept in the inter-relationship between the status and ranked groups of the Johari Bhotias. This has led to the loosening and weakening of the pervasiveness of the economic basis of rank-stratification in the Bhotia society. The Bharet Bhotias, until the closure of the trade, enjoyed a superior economic and ritualistic status over the Kunkiya and Nitwal Bhotias. The Kunkiya and Nitwal Bhotias, due to their economic backwardness, were the subordinates of the Bharet Bhotias. These two endogamous and status groups were largely dependent upon the Bharet Bhotias for their subsistence. But, after the termination of the trade, the Bharet Bhotias, who found themselves in a difficult position for earning a sound and regular income, could not afford to support these two groups as earlier. As a result of these constraints, the ties of economic interdependence and interrelationship between the three status groups got broke up and disintegrated. In the present day Bhotia Society, these three status groups are leading an independent socio-economic life, though the stigma and privilege of ritual pollution and purity still persists with them.

These three groups amongst the Johari Bhotias still practise the endogemic rules strictly. However, some stray cases of marriage between a Kunkiya and a Bharet individual, and vice-versa have also been found. But such cases are extremely few and do not help in the direction of trend setting. Some Kunkiya boys and girls who have managed to obtain higher education and get absorbed in the white-collar jobs, have started drawing attention of the parents of Bharet Bhotias. Now, they think in terms of, though with a hitch, procuring spouses from among the literate and well-to-do Kunkiya and Nitwal families. But, such Bharet Bhotia families are too few in number because they are condemnned by other Bharet Bhotia families for obtaining spouses of Kunkiya status. All this has thus resulted in, even after the 17 years of change in the socio-economic conditions of Bhotias, the persistence of the rank-stratified society amongst the Johari Bhotias.

EXTERNAL SOCIAL RELATIONS

The cessation of Bhotias' trade with Tibet has also brought significant changes in the relationships of the Bhotias with their neighbouring peoples. During the trade economy, the Bhotias maintained relationship with their neighbouring people mainly on two grounds :

(i) for carrying out internal trade, and

(ii) a tenant-owner relationship.

After the disruption of the trade, both these two elements on which Bhotias' relationship with their satellite groups like Thakur, Brahman, Jethora and others was based, has changed considerably. Not only the internal trade of the Bhotias was completely paralysed, but the tenant-owner relationship was also disrupted. While the reason for the dwindling of Bhotias' internal trade has already been discussed earlier, reason behind the change in the tenant-owner relationships with regard to land tenure, deserves discussion. Since the Bhotias were the absentee landlords of their land holdings, after the implementation of the Zamindari Abolition Act of 1961, they had to surrender their land holdings to their 'sirtans' (tenant-cultivators). Thus, the relationship of tenant-owner was changed and the tenants of the Bhotias became the 'hissedar' (proprietor) of the Bhotias' land holdings. Now-a-days, when the Bhotias are leading a settled life in the villages of their winter-settlements, they see with profound grief landholdings are being exploited and cultivated by the local 'jimidars' (agriculturist) who were, until recently, their tenant cultivators. This has, naturally, resulted in the development of a sort of jealous nature among Bhotias for their neighbouring peasants. These days the Bhotias envy the local peasants and are having a constrained relations with them.

Besides all this, the other important element which has cropped up in the external social relationship of Bhotias, is the increase in the acculturative influences. Prior to the cessation of the trade, Bhotias were having only casual social relations with the local peasants who are predominantly Hindu. But this casual social relationship has now turned into a perpetual social relationship because of the sedentraization of the migratory Bhotias. Due to this, now a days, Bhotias are living in a constant company of the Hindu people and, thus, also are becoming increasingly acculturated and Hinduised.

EDUCATION

It has already been noted earlier that Bhotias, during their trade economy, paid little emphasis on the value of education. Until recently there were a few graduates and post-graduates in the Johar Bhotia society. But there has been a tremendous change in the educational status of the Bhotias in the last one and a half decades. After the closure of the trade, the Bhotias gave up their migratory life and paid considerable attention towards the education of their children. Such a trend got momentum due to two main reasons :

i) Carving out Pithoragarh from Almora as a separate district in the year 1960.

ii) Bhotias being made Scheduled Tribe in the year 1967.

As a part of district development measures, the authorities took special care in terms of opening schools and colleges in the Bhotia region, which were conspicuously lacking in the pre-1960 period. At present the Munsiari tehsil, an administrative sub-division in the Bhotia region, is having the following educational institutions :

Institution	*No.*
Government Inter College	1
Government High School (Boys)	4
Government High School (Girls)	1
Government Junior High School	7
Government Primary School (Boys)	71
Government Primary School (Girls)	5
Government Residential School (Boys)	1
Total :	90

Source of data : Block Development Office, Munsiari Block.

All these Schools have been opened in the Bhotia region in the post-1960 period. In the present survey of Bhotia people, five educational institutions of Bhotia region were investigated to find out the participation of Bhotia students. From the Table 16, one can have an idea about the distribution of Bhotia students in the different educational institutions. It is clear from the table that in all these institutions, Bhotia students have shown an edge over the people of other caste groups. In some institutions Bhotias are also serving as teachers. Besides the opening of the educational institutions in the Bhotia region, the other contributing factor is the financial aid and reservations for admission in the educational institutions, which the Bhotias have started getting after 1967 due to being declared as the Schedule Tribe. Now-a-days one can find that Bhotias are having education in the different fields viz. arts, science, engineering, medicine, education, etc. Bhotias have

TABLE—16

Distribution of Bhotia Students in the Schools and Colleges of Munsiari Tahsil

Sl. no.	Educational Institution	Class held	Co-ed Boys or Girls	No. of Bhotia teachers	Total Strength	Specification of Students: Male Bhotia	Male Harijan	Male Other Caste	Female Bhotia	Female Harijan	Female Other Caste
1.	Govt. Inter College (1961)	6th Cl. to 12th Cl.	Co-Ed.	3	518	280 (54.05%)	27	110	46	2	53
2.	Govt. High School (1965)	1st Cl. to 11th Cl.	Girls	6	110	–	—	—	98	10	2
3.	Basic Pr. School (1959) Dummer	1st Cl. to 5th Cl.	Co-Ed.	—	81	19 (23.46%)	17	10	23	10	2
4.	Basic Pr. School Munsiari (1961)	Do	Do	—	177	37 (20.90%)	31	28	42	16	17
6.	Ashram Padhdhiti (Residential School-1973)	6th Cl. to 8th Cl.	Boys	—	82	63 (76.83%)	19	—	—	—	—
	Total				968	399 (41.23%)	94	148	209	38	74

(Source : Attendance registers of the institutions).

TABLE—17

Educational Standard Amongst the Bhotias

Sl. No.	Population Sex	No	Illiterate	Literate	Educational Standard Primary	Middle	Intermediate	Graduate	Post Graduate
1.	Male	545	137 (25.11%)	408(74.84%)	165(30%)	95(17.43%)	109(20%)	31(5.69%)	18(3.3%)
1.	Female	472	226(47.43%)	246(52.12%)	117(24.91%)	60(12.71%)	37(7.37%)	20(4.23%)	2(.46%)
Total :		1017	363(35.69%)	654(64.39%)	282(27.82%)	155(15.24%)	146(14.35%)	5 (5.01%)	20(1.08%)

not only confined themselves to their own region, but they have also crossed their geographical boundary for taking higher education. In the present survey it was found that the Bhotia boys and girls were taking education in the distant places like Lucknow, Allahabad, Kanpur, Agra, Delhi etc. All this has naturally put Bhotias in the category of various white collar jobs like Doctor, Engineer, Magistrate, Administrator, teachers, etc. Now-a-days it is not uncommon to find one doctor, engineer, teacher etc. from and in almost each Bhotia village. It can be safely concluded that this breakthrough in Bhotia education has come due to the transformation in the economic system which was based on the Indo-Tibetan trade. The trading economy of the Bhotias was characterized by semi-nomadic and a transhumant life. It is held beyond all shadows of doubt that a settled life is more suited for the pursuit of educational knowledge than a migratory life. And such a situation is clearly disernible in the case of Bhotia society, From the Table 17, one can see the educational status of Bhotia people which is based on the data derived from the survey of 12 Bhotia villages.

POLITICAL ORGANISATION

In the traditional Bhotia society, the unit of social control was the village. Each Bhotia village had its headman (Padhan). The duties of the 'Padhan' mainly pertained to act as :

i) Revenue Collector, and settlement,

ii) trade–taxes collector, and

iii) sacred specialist.

Of all these duties, the collection of trade taxes and acting as the sacred specialist were the most important. But after the stoppage of the trade and introduction of the "Panchayati Raj" in India, the traditional political organisation of the Bhotias has undergone considerable changes. Now-a-days the only traditional element of the Bhotias' political organization is reflected in the role of the 'Padhan' as a sacred specialist. The modern village-heads are known as 'Sabhapati', and the revenue—collector as Patwari. This way, it is found that in a Bhotia village, there are two village authorities (i)-the *Padhan*, whose post is hereditary, and (ii) the *Sabhapati*, who is officially elected once in every five years. The traditional village-head-the Padhan, looks after the religious affairs of the village. The modern village-head—the Sabhapat,—maintains law and order within his jurisdiction in the village.

Prior to the cessation of the trade, a Bhotia 'Padhan' was to act as the revenue collector. But such a work was seldom enjoyed by the Bhotia traders because it used to involve lot of time without any substantial gain. Bhotias were quite reluctant to do any work other than those which brought dividend in terms of money. But still the Bhotias were doing job of revenue collector because of the administrative considerations. Although such a work did attach some social prestige to the individual Bhotia 'Padhan' and his clan members, it was in no sense considered better than the prestige which was achieved on account of economic prosperity. That is why the Bhotias accepted the change in the power of revenue collector in the post 1962 period without any retaliation. In the present times, the relationship between the traditional 'Padhan', now only a sacred specialist, of Bhotias and the modern village head or 'Sabhapati' is quite cordial, amicable, and fully adjusted.

Subsequent to the stoppage of the trade, Bhotias have also developed interest in the village polity which is based on the line principles of 'Panchayati Raj' in India.

In the Munsiari tehsil a Block Development Office was established in the year 1956. In this block there are nine 'NYAY-PANCHAYAT' which comprises 76 "GRAM-SABHA(S)". Each 'Nyay-Panchayat' and 'Gram-Sabha' has a '*Sarpanch*' and 'Gram-Pradhan' or 'Sabhapati' respectively. In the present survey it was found that out of 9 Nyay-Panchayat in the Munsiari Block of Bhotia region, 3 Sarpanchs belongs to Bhotia community. Similarly, out of 76 Gram Sabhas, 29 Gram-Pradhans belonged to Bhotia community, and 47 belonged to other caste groups. Again, it was also found that out of 10 VLW (Village Level Workers) in Munsiari Block, 3 VLWs belonged to Bhotia community. All these figure clearly show that, even in the changed socio-economic and socio-political situations, Bhotias are playing a significant role in the village and block level political organization.

CO-OPERATIVE SOCIETIES

Prior to the cessation of the trade, Bhotias were having a number of co-operative societies which were based on the clan level, status-group level and community level. But after the cessation of the trade, all such co-operative societies of Bhotias either *became extinct or dys*-functional. However, in the changed economic conditions, some active Bhotia people have managed to open some new co-operative societies which are successfully working in the Bhotia region. In the present time, there are three co-operatives in the Bhotia society. They are :

i) Bunkar Udyog Samiti,

ii) Sadhan Sahkari Samiti, and

iii) Bahuddesiya Janjati Samiti.

As is evident from the name, these co-operative societies of Johari Bhotias are catering to different needs of Johari Bhotias. Bhotias can obtain wool at cheaper rate from these societies and can also sell the finished woollen materials. Besides supplying wool, these societies are also supplying clothes, cotton yarn, food-grains etc. But there are some fundamental differences in the nature of these cooperative societies and those which were functioning earlier i.e. before 1962. While the old co-operative societies were mostly individualistic i.e. in nature based on status group and clans, the new ones are communal. Any Bhotia, irrespective of the membership, can obtain things from these Sahkari Samities.

RELIGION

For the last several centuries the Bhotias' religion has been exposed to the influence of theTibetan and the Hindu traditions. Hence their religion carries the stamp of both the religions. Due to their trade economy, which involved semi-nomadism, the Bhotias quite often come into contact with the peoples of Buddhist and Hindu religious background. While the trade with the Tibetans has been responsible for the influence of Buddhism, the trade with the pahari people imbibed the elements of Hinduism on the religious beliefs and practice of Bhotias. But the stoppage of the trade with Tibet, and the consequent changes in the economic activities and settlement pattern, have considerably influenced the body of reli gious beliefs and practices.

It has been seen earlier that that the Bhotias, during their trade with Tibet used to perform and celebrate the worshipping of most of their Tibe tan, Hindu, and animistic deities in the villages of summer settlement. It was celebrated and performed in a very organised and elegant manner in the summer settlement because all the Bhotias of one clan were available in one village. Not only the individual clan deity but also the common deity of Bhotias was worshiped at the village level. Even the temples of some of the deities of Bhotias like Nanda Devi, Raga, Manhfaila, Shankh, etc. are situated in the village of summer settlement. the Mana wall of the Johari Bhotias, which carried the Tibetan mantra-OM MANE PADME HUM, was also confined to the dwelling of only summer settlement. But after the cessation of the trade, the Bhotias abandoned or deserted the dwelling of their summer settlement and got settled in the villages of winter and intermediate settlement. This led to the proliferation of Bhotia clans into different villages and some mixed clan villages. All this had two distinct effects on the religious life of the Bhotias. Firstly, the Bhotias got cut-off from the Tibetans and hence also from their religious intercourse, and due to the abandonment of the summer villages the influence of

Mana walls also lost and nowadays such walls carry a barren look in the dilapidated dwellings of the summer settlement. Secondly, due to the sedentarization in the downhill villages, the Bhotias have now developed a perpetual social relations with the local peasant castes who are predominantly Hindus. The Bhotias, who claim to have a Hindu descendance and call themselves as Rajputs, have thus got themselves compelled to conform to the norms and values of Hinduism.These days their socio-cultural ceremonies like marriage, birth, death-rites etc. are being observed strictly on the line of the Hindu traditions. There is hardly any socio-religious function of Bhotias, which is performed in the absence of the Brahmin (ritual priest). The other element of Bhotias' religion which has witnessed change, is the mode of worshipping of clan deity and common deities. In the bygone days i.e., before 1962 the worshipping of the deities was done in very organised manner which reflected the enthusiasm and gay spirit of Bhotias. But in the persent time, the clan deity is worshipped at family level and the common deities are worshipped at village level. Some Bhotias who have got settled in the semi-urban and urban environment, have become completely isolated and detached from the mainstream of their community's religious values and ethos. Such Bhotias have either stopped propitiating some deities or have modified the way of appeasement. The deities like Nanda Devi, Raga, Shankh, etc., whose temples were situated in the villages of summer settlements, are now worshipped in the downhill villages. Bhotias have made new temples of their respective clan deities and common deities. Naturally, with the change in the temple's place, the spirit of devotion has also gone down. However, despite such changes in the elements of Bhotias religion, the role of their traditional village headman (Padhan) as performer of the sacred rites, has not changed. The most important change is manifest in the cessation of the celebration of the religious festival like *Saubali*, *Ghiyutyo-her*, *Bhoot-pitra-chechet* etc. The celebration of these festivals was done in the summer settlements and now after its abandonment, such festivals have become completely out of practice.

Again it is found that due to the stoppage of the trade, there has been certain distinct changes in the religious fairs of the Bhotias. It has been seen earlier that the religious fairs of the Johari Bhotias e.g., Jauljibi, Thal, and Bageshwar fairs, were more of commercial importance than religious, have now lost its glory and importance. The Bhotias used to sell out their imported goods in these fairs. But with the cessation of the trade, the import of the goods such as borax, wool, Tibetan salt, ponies etc. was also stopped. Nowadays, besides the woollen products from their own woollen industry, Bhotias have nothing else to sell in these fairs. Hence, the participation of Bhotias in these fairs have gone down considerably which has made these fairs merely a religious gathering of a thin crowd.

ADAPTIVE PROCESSES

Human systems are not unitary, but dynamic and proliferational. When needs cannot be satisfied by one system, then a sub-system is formed through the adaptive actions of individuals or group. Sometime the individuals or group switch the behaviour from one system, or sub-systems to another for seeking out more congenial alternatives. But why and when individuals or groups are required to effect changes in the patterned behaviour ? The simple answer is due to forces of changes. When any novelty alters the patterned behaviour of the group, then the individuals adopt the alteration in the system by making responsive changes. For any long term or short term fluctuations in the patterned system, corresponding changes in the structures or its components must be made. The individual or group may adapt by finding new solutions to new or old problems ; or it may adapt by simply learning to live with the existing situation. But the adaptive systems are dynamic systems, because the innovative solutions to problems tend to create new problems, which must be coped with future date. The present study leads to an appreciation for the varieties of adaptations that have enabled Bhotias to survive in the wake of the problems arising out of the transformation in the economic system.

It has been noted earlier that the trading activities of Bhotias have been closely attuned to their socio-cultural life. Almost each economic and social activity was somehow related to the Indo-Tibetan trade of the Bhotias. Bhotia people have shown a remarkable degree of competence to blend with the local environment. In the different regions, varying patterns of adaptations are to be seen. They created apporpriate institutions to satisfy their needs. The social organization was adjusted to the different demands of these tasks, not only from one settlement to another, but seasonally within the same environment. The adaptive strategies of Bhotias have clearly shown that there is a close relationship between the subsistence techniques and social organization. The case of Bhotia society has also manifested the importance of cultural flexibility as an adaptive strategy. The Bhotias borrowed techniques and technologies from other people with whom they came into contact and adapted them to suit the demands of their environment. It is the accommodation which greatly facilitated their survival in an extremely difficult and inhospitable environment. But it is seen that some adaptive strategies of Bhotia have certain undesirable and unhealthy effects on the long term social situations. The innovative solultions which the Bhotias had evolved to cope with the land exploitative system and to cope with the immediate problem faced by the closure of the trade, have created new socio-economic problems. It has been noted earlier that due to the heavy involvement in the trading activities, the Bhotias could not devote themselves to agricultural activities and, hence they had given their lands to the local peasant castes for exploitation on share crop basis. Though such a land tenure system of Bhotias functioned with gainful returns until 1961, it had disastrous effect on the land holdings of the Bhotias in the future date. Subsequent to the introduction of the Zamindari

Abolition Act, 1961, Bhotias were deprived of a major part of their land holding. Thus, after the closure of the trade relations with Tibet, Bhotias were not able to fall back on agriculture as their main element of subsistence activities. Similarly, it was noted that to cope with the problems posed immediately after the cessation of trade, the Bhotias obtained cash money by selling out their flocks—sheep, goats, mules ponies, etc. Though such strategic actions helped Bhotias to pull on for a year or two without bothering much for subsistence, it had tremendous effect on the woollen industry of the Bhotias. The supply of wool was not only stopped from Tibet but the local administration also put certain restrictions in terms of procuring wool from Nepal, Tibet (through Nepal), and other sources. Thus, the shortage of wool hit hard the prospects of Bhotias' woollen industry. They were forced to depend entirely on the Khadi Gram Udyog Commission for procuring wool and thus also selling the finished product. The income derived from such a restrained woollen industry has served only as the palliative for the Bhotias. Had Bhotias maintained their own sheep flocks, they would not have faced such a grim situation in running their woollen industry.

By far, however, the most important significance of an evaluative study of adaptive processes of Bhotia society, lies in the fact that it warrants the human society for not depending entirely on a trade and commerce which is based on the delicate link between the political frontiers and policies of two or more countries. Any conflict between the two countries may disturb the entire socio-economic set-up. The Bhotia society provides a burning example of such a situation. They depended mainly on the trade with Tibet for their subsistence. Their whole socio-economic life was moulded in the frame of a trade economy. But despite several trade treaties between the two countries, the Bhotias' trade was finally stopped. The stoppage of the trade, as seen earlier, necessitated Bhotias to reorientate their socio-economic life. These changes, which have crept in the Bhotia society, have entirely altered the life-style of the Bhotia community. From a non-sedentary trading community they have been forced to adopt an entirely new way of life. Their social organization, that had developed and crystallized over centuries had adapted itself to a particular environment and ecology which had also shaped their economic structure due to their geographical position. But suddenly, the economic, structure which may be regarded as the basis of the Bhotias' social structure, crumbled and along with the whole edifice of Bhotia life changed. A society that undergoes such a vertical change cannot immediately cope with the problems of new situation. It takes at least three generations to adapt and maintain a viable relationship with the new situation. This is so because a sudden gust of unplanned and unprecedented changes bring with it a lot of problems, which are not merely economic, but primarily social and psychological.

A study of the adaptive processes of Bhotia, which have emerged after the cessation of the trade, reflects three distinct varieties of adaptation. As conceived by W.J. Berry (1966), they are (1) *Adjustment*, (2) *Reaction* and (3) *Withdrawal*. In the present study of Bhotia society, all those families who have got settled themselves in their two settlements winter and intermediate settlements, and are following a diverse type of occupations for subsistence, represent the *adjustment mode of adaptation*. This is so because such families have changed their behaviour by bringing it into harmony with the environment. They have learned to live with the existing situation or prevailing reality. The *Reaction type of adaptation* is represented by those Bhotia families who still migrate to the villages of their summer settlement stay there for about three to four months in the monotonous situation and practise cultivation. Such Bhotia families (30 out of 224) are still retaliating and struggling with the changed environment and, thus, it is seen that they have not been able to increase the congruence between their behaviour and the changed environment. The third variety of adaptation i.e., *The Withdrawal*, is represented by those families who, after the cessation of their trans-Himalayan trade, have got settled themselves in the semi-urban and urban environment which are altogether different from the socio-economic environment of Bhotias. Though such Bhotia families (80 out of 224) are leading a well-to-do life, they correspond to the withdrawal variety of adaptation because they have withdrawn themselves from the adaptive arena, i.e. the Johar valley. However, the overall assessment of the adaptive processes of Bhotias reveal that out of 224 Bhotia families, 49.11% Bhotia families are well adjusted, 15.18% Bhotia families are still retaliating to the change, and 35.71% Bhotia families are though well adjusted to the change, they are no more a part of the adaptive arena because of their withdrawal.

PROBLEM OF REHABILITATION

To maintain that the Bhotias are a prosperous people, in the present condition is a serious myth which must be exploded. To regard them as uncivilized and barbarous is equal to accrue an insult to their culture which has accommodated different socio-cultural elements from time to time. They are accommodating enough to take a new skill and technique, and have enough sense to judge what is good and not. And above all they are spurred with the desire to pull and push through. But, in the last one and a half decade, Bhotias have faced a very traumatic socio-economic condition. Prior to the Chinese occupation of Tibet, the backbone of the economy of the Bhotia people was trade with Tibet from which they have drawn sustenances through generations. The cessation of trade relations with Tibet has completely shattered the economy of the Bhotias and has broken down the self-sufficiency of the inhabitants of this mountainous country. The transition from trade to agriculture and a commercial economy based on local sources, has caused much discomforts and economic problems for the Bhotias.

To sum up, the Bhotia community is experiencing an acute sense of economic, social and cultural insecurity.

Nothing less than a comprehensive programme of rehabilitation is required to pull them through the crucial stage of social and economic transitions and help them to adjust to new persuits and new way of life, so that they could rise to the occasion in the case of an eventuality. Hence, the rehabilitation scheme in the Bhotia region, a regicn which has great strategic importance for the entire nation, should be so guided and directed that the suffering of the Bhotias could be avoided. However, the rehabilitation scheme should centre principally round the economic activities because this will check the progressively deteriorating economic conditions.

Rehabilitation of the Bhotia economy should not only include agricultural practices with the help of the regional commercial scurces, but should be guided by various silvicultural and horticultural programmes so that the Bhotia traders may find out an adequate living by depending on them. This is possible only when Bhòtias can adapt their mode of living and agricultural practices to the changed conditions and also if they can be assured of proper prices for their products. Besides introducing some new techniques, it would be desirable that a thorough scientific change in the already existing techniques of their traditional occupations, such as woollen industry and sheep rearing. In the pre-1962 period, besides trade, the economic structure of the Bhotias was characterized by a unique predominance of cottage industries. In the cottage industry, the spinning and weaving of wool into rugs, carpets, and various other woollen articles were of greatest importance and the products found a market in fair and other terai and hill market centres. Bhotias have traditionally been excellent craftsmen of the woollen industry and have acquired a fair degree of skill. But, in the present times, this industry is facing a lot of problems due to a variety of reasons. No steps have been taken to modernize the age-old Bhotia woollen cottage industry. Though the Bhotia people have gained considerable reputation for their woollen carpets, rugs, shawls, etc., the articles produced by them are not sophisticated enough to capture the market in the urban centres of Kumaon and plains. They still spin and weave with their age-old techniques, which not only affects the quality of the finished products but also reduces their quantity. In fact, the technique of production needs a scientific change so that the quality is improved and larger-scale production is made possible.

In recent years, the Uttar Pradesh Government has taken a number of steps during the Development Plan Periods, which include setting up of weaving plants, wool training-cum-production centres, wool utilisation centres and sale depots, etc. at different places. But, the actual implementation of such scheme suffers from various problems, that are invariably local in nature and necessitates an appraisal in view of the peculiar environmental condition. The basic factor involved is that of distances and the peripheral location of the present centres is far from most of the Bhotia villages which are situated in the interiors. In such a region of rugged terrain, where transport and communication facilities are too meagre or non-existing, emphasis should have been laid towards setting up the training, marketing or production centres within easy reach of a group of settlements, if not for individual village. Further, it is quite impreratïve that the woollen products of Bhotias should find a ready market through wide publicity at various urban centres of Kumaon which are frequented by tourists from all over the country. This will result into a great demand for the products and a much wider publicity on a national level. This can be made possible by setting up separate show-rooms for these people at the towns, subsidised or aided by the government. Similarly, the question of a proper distribution of the produce is no less significant since it vitally enters into considerations of profits of the Bhotia manufacturers and, thus, ultimately the success of the industry. To achieve this, it is incumbent upon the authorities to create a co-operative system wherein all the materials manufactured by Bhotias may be collected for proper distribution among sale-depots, show-rooms, and the like. This will create a regulated system of supply and may go a long way in ensuring a fair amount of profit in the industry.

The next important aspect to be considered is that of improvement in the existing techniques of production, so that the quality of the product could be improved. In order to effect large-scale production, the necessity of mechanised techniques of production cannot be over-emphasised. This is important for capturing a market and competing in the international carpet markats. In order to accomplish this, it would be desirable to train the Bhotias in improved techniques. These days the educated Bhotia girls are developing a reluctant attitude towards their cottage industry. They feel that such a work are not up to the mark for educated girls. Such a motivation deserves a proper modification. In this respect the type of education imparted to the Bhotia children plays an important role. Besides the teaching of usual subjects, there should be some orientation for imparting education in the field of handicrafts.

By far, however, the most important porblem that Bhotias are facing with regard to their woollen industry pertains to the acute shortage of raw material. Since the supply of raw wool from Tibet has been cut-off, the Bhotias are now solely dependant on the insufficient quantity of wool supplied by the Khadi Gram Udyog Commission and on the meagre supply of wool from their own flocks. The wool obtained from their own flocks is of an inferior quality and makes coarse and rough woollen articles only. Moreover, the scheme of supplying wool to the Bhotia under the development programmes is not a permanent measure to cope with the demand. In order to ensure a fair and regular supply of wool to the Bhotias, there can be perhaps no better alternative than a systematic sheep-farming which, fortunately, has been an integral part of the Bhotias' economy. With proper incentive, guidance and financial aid, they (Bhotias) can produce enough wool for their requirements. Under the circumstances, therefore, it appears to be the only permanent solution of their economic crisis. In this direction it would, however, be essential on the part of the authorities to guide the people to resort to a controlled grazing on a rotational basis and to provide them with better breeds of flocks, cross-breeding of the indigenous breeds with the good wool producing sheep breed. The government should also allot grazing grounds to these people in the foothill areas where they can go with the flocks during the winter. Though these facilities exist and are being provided to the Bhotias, but, the nature of the problems demands a greater and more sympathetic attention.

6

Conclusion

In the foregoing chapters I have discussed the Bhotias' society in its historical and contemporary situation. From the detalied account of the dynamics of change and adaptation in the Bhotia society, certain derivations have been made. I have tried to fit the findings of this study in the light of the theoretical concepts which have been outlined in the Introduction chapter. While discussing the derivations of the study, I am also inclined to consider it in the light of the different hypotheses which were envisaged in the begining. In the discussion which follows, it will be seen that most of the hypotheses have been found in conformity with the findings of this study. The type of study which is presented here has two aspects—firstly, a theoretical one of trying to understand what is the place of mankind in a proliferational and dynamic society, and secondly, how well adapted is man to the dynamic characterstic of the society. The importance of such a study consists in presenting a comprehensive picture of a slice of human society in its diachronic situation. If this is done accurately and comprehensively, such a presentation remains of permanent value. In order to achieve this, the Bhotia society has been studied and an attempt is made here to describe its changing frontiers of socio-cultural elements in the best possible manner.

The treatise on Bhotia tribe is focussed mainly on the principal element of the Bhotias' economic organisation. It analyses that how one single economic component, which is the main pillar of an economic system, influences and determines the other economic elements and the entire course of socio-cultural life. It also examines that how a change in the main component of the economic system, leads to corresponding changes in its correlated parts. And when the change is sudden, then the community undergoing such a dynamics of change faces adaptational problems at various levels.

Among all the elements of the economic organisation of Bhotias, the Indo-Tibetan trade was the principal economic activity. The other economic activities, such as the trade with the 'pahari' people, agriculture, pastoralism, and woollen industry, etc. were associated with and dependent on the Tibetan trade of the Bhotias. The mountainous terrrain of the Bhotia abode, half of which is snow-bound for almost half of the year and the other half not being very arable due to the physical and climatic conditions, forced the Bhotias to pursue an occupation other than agriculture. This leads us to conclude that the dependence of the Bhotias on the trans-Himalayan trade is neither of their own choosing nor it is the result of historic accident. A self-contained peasant economy based on agriculture and natural husbandary could not be sustained from the natural resources of the region. Such a subsistence strategy of the Bhotias helps us in understanding the interrelationship of environment, subsistence, and society. It also leads us conclude that every culture has inherent in its system a strategy of adaptation through which people make effective use of their environment under different circumstances. As a culture experiences its environment, the behaviour system will be shaped by that experience.

The trading methods of the Bhotia with Tibetans were based on barter and mutual faith. Such a system gave birth to many customs like, 'Sulchyu-milchyu'. 'Gamgia', 'Sarji', etc. These customs are not only unique but also very significant because such customs are becoming extinct. The 'Sulchyu-milchyu' custom, which initiated friendhsip between two trade partners, finds its parallel in the economic institutions like 'Kula-exchange', and 'Potlatch, of the Trobriand Islanders. The Bhotia and the Tibetan trade partners, after initiating a trade relationahip, used to exchange gifts with each other. In the present day economic institutions which are based on a highly complicated processes and competitive attitudes, the simple trading system between Bhotia and the Tibetans, throws a new light on the mercantile culture and entreprenurial courage.

The detailed study of the economic organisation of the Bhotias shows that how in a society one particular economic activity may have its deep rooted repercussions on the other economic activities. Bhotias, due to their heavy involvement in the trans-Himalayan trade, could not cultivate their lands and resorted to share-cropping. Similarly, the woollen industry of the Bhotias, until 1962, largely flourished in the backdrop of the raw wool imported from Tibet. The flocks of the Bhotias, which consisted of sheep, goat, mules, etc, were used mainly as beasts of burden, facilitated Bhotias in carrying out their trade operations. This way it is seen that the pastoral economy of the Bhotias was also closely attuned to the trade economy formed the principal element of Bhotias' economic structure. Such a system in which the economic elements are co-existent and dependent on one particular economic element, provides us with a picture of human society which is a closely integrated empirical system. And, thus, it lends support to the theoretical proposition of Sorokin (1941) who says, "If a given culture is the co-existence of several systems and co-existence of one single congeries within or outside the system, then all its important elements and components united into one system or supersystem or supersystems change together as parts of the whole." The Bhotia society very closely conforms to such a situation. After the cessation of the trade which has been the main element of the Bhotias' economy, there has been changes in almost all the economic elements and in the socio-cultural elements. While some of the elements have undergone profound changes, certain elements have been reorientated and modified.

Bhotias carried out trade with Tibet for last several centuries. But external factors, especially political developments, have always been important cause for bringing about changes in the patterned system of a society. Due to the interference of external forces Bhotias had to lose their trade with Tibet which was assiduously built up and passed on from generation to generation. Until the occupation of Tibet by Chinese forces in 1959, the Bhotias maintained a flourishing trade relations with Tibet. But, with the change in the political set-up in Tibet, the Bhotias found themselves faced with the serious problem of losing their age-old occupation. The Chinese began interfering in their traditional trade with the Tibetans. Despite the Sino-Indian agreement of 1954 and several other trade treaties, the Bhotias' trade situation worsened and in 1962, with the Chinese aggression on India, it was completely stopped. All this situation leads us to infer that there always exists a disequilibrium tendency between a social system and its environment.

The termination ot the trade relations of Bhotias with Tibet through the political events outside their control, has had profound effects on the entire way of Bhotias' socio-cultural life. It not only forced Bhotias to reorientate their economic system, but also necessitated them to effect change in the elements of its social life. The settlement pattern, family and household organisation, social stratification, etc. of Bhotia people have been intimately related with the trading activities of the Bhotias. After the cessation of the trade, the Bhotias effected changes in their erstwhile economic elements, and also adopted new economic activities like contract taking, liquor vending, Government service, etc. Similarly, after the stoppage of the trade, it has been noted that Bhotias gave up a seminomadic life, deserted their summer settlement villages, started a sedentary life, effected change in the composition of family, readjusted their relationship with the different status groups of their community, and also with the people of the neighbouring peasant castes, etc. All these changes which have crept in the Bhotia society have got their roots in only one single element i.e., the trade. Hence, it can be concluded that any serious change in the important elements or part of socio-cultural system results in simultaneous change in the correlated parts of the system. The study also discloses that the pursuance of trade as a central economic activity has had considerable influence on the social attitudes, structure, and organisation of the Bhotia people.

After the closure of the trade, Bhotias adopted a multitude of economic activities such as shopkeeping, contract taking, liquor vending, etc. These economic activities constitute main occupation of the Bhotias in their post-transformation i.e., transformation in the main pillar of the economy, period. It can be seen that such economic activities, as have emerged after the closure of the trade, are more commercial than agricultural in nature. Doesn't it help in building a notion that people motivated by a specific outlook are more likely to achieve success in adopting occupations of similar nature then those conditioned by a different ideology ? Such a situation becomes amply manifested in the case of the Bhotia society.

The study of Bhotia society shows that from time immemorial, Bhotia people have been effecting effective adjustments to different situations. Bhotia people have showed a remarkable degree of competence to blend with the varying patterns of environment. In the different regions varying patterns of adaptations are to be seen. They created appropriate institutions to satisfy their needs. The social organisation of Bhotias was adjusted to the different demands of these tasks. The case of Bhotia society has also manifested the importance of cultural flexibility as an adaptive strategy. The Bhotias borrowed techniques and technologies from other peoples with whom they came in contact and adapted them suit the demands of their environments. It is the accommodation which greatly facilitated their survival in an extremely difficult and inhospitable environment. The study of Bhotia society, thus, clearly shows that man's social life is modified in adaptation to the demands inherent in his cultural equipment and related techniques. After the closure of the trade, the Bhotias had to face a traumatic situation in terms of seeking alternative sources of livelihood and modifying the social life in conformity to the economic constraints. While many Bhotia families abandoned their home village and moved down to lower regions to seek alternative sources of livelihood, quite a good number of Bhotia families are still struggling and retaliating with their changed environment. All Bhotia families are making their best efforts to adapt to their changed environment and obtain a viable economic base from among the limited regional potentialities and cut-throat competition.

Bhotias are nowadays trapped, due to the dynamics of economic transformation, in a complex social situation. A situation in which a Bhotia is a link of cultural continuity between his ascendents and descendents. He has been socialized by the former and is ready to socialize the latter. He makes many a daily adjustmen and thereby indicates that no adaptation is permanent.

Bibliography

Akhandanand, Swami 1938 *Tibbater Pathe Himalaya.* Uttodhan Karyalaya. Calcutta. (original version published in 1904 in Uttbodhan)

Alland, Alexander (Jr.) 1975 *Adaptation.* In Annual Review of Anthropology. Vol. 4. California.

Apurbanand, Swami 1966 *Kailash abong Manas-Tirthayatra.* Hindi Translation : Kailash aur Manas-Tirtha-Yatra Varanashi: Ramakrishna Adwaitashram (Translated from Bengali by Gopal Chandra Vedantashastri).

Ashbey William R. 1956 *An Introduction To Cybernetics.* Wiley. New York.

Atkinson, E.R. 1882 *Economic Mineralogy of The Hill Districts of N.W.P.* Allahabad : Government Press.

Atkinson, E.T. 1882 *The Himalayan Districts of North Western Provinces of India.* Vol. I. Allahabad. Vol. II. Allahabad

1886 Vol XII-*Gazetteer of the North-Provinces and Oudh.* Allahabad.

Auden, J.B.	1937	*The Structure Of The Himalayas in Garhwal.* Calcutta.
Bagchi, Gourchandra	1977	*Miscellaneous note : Some socio-economic aspects of stratification in the East Himalayan society,* Man in India, 57 (4), 363-367.
Bahadur, K.P.	1978	*Castes, Tribes And Culture of India.* Vol. 5. Uttar Pradesh. Es Es Publications. New Delhi.
Banerjee, M.	1964	*The Bhot People. Primitive Men In India.* Ambala.
Banerjee, Nitynarayan		*The Himalayas.* Calcutta.
Bapna Devilal	1978	*Uttarakhand Mein Bharat Ke Akhri Gaon Tak* (In Hindi). In. Hindustan (a Hindi). May 19, 1978. New Dehli.
Batten, J.H.	1851	*Official Reports On The Province Of Kumaon.* Government Press. Agra (includes the classic statistical sketch of Kumaon, by G.W Traill, 1820).
Beckett, J.O.B., and Ramsay, Sir H.	1874	*Reports On The Revision Of Settlement in Kumaon Districts,* Government Press. Allahabad.
Backett, J.O.B.	1886	*Reports on the Settlement In Garhwal District.* Government Press, Allahabad.
Bennet, W. John.	1976	*The Ecological Transition.* Pergamon Press. New York.
Berreman, G.D.	1960	*Cultural Variability And Drift In The Himalayan Hills.* American Anthropologist. 6 2, 774-94.

	1963	*Hindus Of The Himalayas.* Univ. of California Press.
Berrier, F. Kenneth.	1968	*General And Social Systems.* Rutgers University Press. New Brunswick.
Berry, W.J.	1976	*Human Ecology And Cognitive Style.* Comparative Studies In Cultural and Psychological Adaptation. Halsted Press. New York.
Bhatnagar, G.S.	1971	*Neglect Of Hill Region Leads To Separatist Movement.* Profile of Backwardness: VII. Times of India. September 13.
Bhatnagar, P.L.	1961	*Bhotia* (Ed.). Census of India 1961. Village Survey Monograph no. 8 : Darkot village, and no. 10 : Ghorpatta Malla village (U.P.) Govt. of India Press, New Delhi.
Bhattacharya, Sunil-Chandra.	1931	*Manas-Sarovar of Kailas,* Basumati Sahitya Mandir, Calcutta.
Biswas, P.C.	1952-53	*Comparative Studies Of The Whorls On Head Hairs of Bhotias, Rajis, Kenets Jaunsaris And Tehri Rajputs.* Eastern Anthropologist. 6 p-106-109.
Blunt, Sir E.A.H.	1952	*Census Report Of The United Provinces of Agra And Oudh,* Part-I.
Bose, Buddha	1954	*Holy Kailash.* Calcutta.
Brahmachari Swami Ramanand	1945	*Kailash Darshan*

Brown, C.W. 1987 *Ecology, Trade and Former Bhotiya Identity,* in M.K. Raha (ed) Himalayan Heritage, Gian Publishing House, Delhi, p 125-138.

Buckley, Walter 1967 *Sociology And Modern Systems Theory.* Prentice Hall, Engelwood Cliffs.

Burman, B.K. Roy 1969 *A Preliminary Appraisal Of The Scheduled Tribes Of India.* Office of the Registrar General of India. New Delhi. p. 33-37.

Burrard, S.G., and Hayden, H.H. 1907 *A Sketch Of The Geography And Geology Or The Himalayas Mountains And Tibet* : Part IV : The Geology of the Himalayas, Govt. of India Press. Calcutta.

Carnac, H.R. 1887 *Ancient Rock Sculpturing In Kumaon.* Calcutta.

Chalk, B.L. 1975 *Kumaon And Garhwal Hill Districts.* Publications Division, New Delhi.

Chandra, Moti 1953 Sartha-Baha. Patna.

Charles, Bell 1968 *The People of Tibet.* Oxford. p. 109-110.

Chatterjee, B.B. 1976 *The Bhotias Of Uttarakhand.* International Centre Quarterly. 3 (1), 3-16.

1977 *Literature On Bhotias Of Kumaon and Garhwal,* Indian Anthropologist. Vol. 7 No. 2, Dec. 77 p. 125-37.

Chatterjee, R.K. 1978 *Indian Land Borders.* Problems And Challenge. Sterling Publishers Pvt. Ltd. New Delhi.

Chatterjee, B.R. *Swadeshi-Bideshe Churashi Bastar Jeevan Japan.* Shri Sharda Press, Calcutta.

Chattopadhaya, Pramode Kumar. 1962 *Himalaya-pare Kailaso O Manas Sarovar.* Orient Book Co., Calcutta.

Clay, J.M. 1915 *Notes On The Bhotias Of British Garhwal.* Typed sheets dated 22-4-1915, in the office of the Dist. Collector, Pauri Garhwal : Reported by Dabral, S.P.

Clive, E.A. 1865 *Bhut Or Bhuttiah. Memorandum On The Prevailing Castes.* Census of North Western Provinces. 1865 Vol, I, General Reports and Appendencies Government Press Allahabad.

Cohen, A. Yehudi 1968 *Man In Adaptation. The Biosocial Background.* Aldine Publishing Co., Chicago.

1971 *Man In Adaptation. The Institutional Framework.* Aldine. New York.

Crooke, W. 1896 *Bhot Bot, Bhotia. The Tribes And Castes of North-Western Provinces And Oudh.* Vol. II. Calcutta.

Dabral, Shiv Prasad 1965 *Alaknanda Upatakya.* Veer Gatha Parkashan Dogadda.

1965 *Uttarakhand Ke Bhotantik.* Veer Gatha Parkashan. Dogadda.

Denelli, Giotto 1933 *Buddhists And Glaciers Of Western Tibet* London.

Das, J.C. 1982 *From Trade to Agriculture, in* K.S. Singh edited "Economics of the Tribes and their Transformation", Concept Publishing Company, New Delhi, p. 208-215.

Das, Sharat Chandra 1902 *Journey To Lhasa And Central Tibet*. London.

Datta Mazumdar, N. 1940 *The Economic Organization Of The Bhotia* Man. (No. 86).

Desideri, Ippolito, S.J., of Pistoia 1931-37 *Tibets Book Of Lungh-ten. The Prophecies Of Urgyen.* (An accouut of travels in Tibet in 1712-1727). London.

Divyatmanand, Swami 1963 *Punyatirtha Bharat.* (*Account of travels of 1941*). Mitra and Ghosh, Calcutta.

Dutt, Sukumar 1962 *Buddhist Monks And Monasteries Of India.* George Allen and Unwin. London

Eisendatt, S.N. 1978 *Revolutions And The Transformation Of Societies.* A Comparative Study of Civilizations. The Free Press. New York.

Eyde, E.H.H. 1921 *Census Of India* Vol. XVI.
1923 *Census Report Of The United Provinces.* Part—I, Bhotia.

Elliot, H.M. 1949 *Races Of North-Western Provinces Of India.* Vol. I. London.

Firth, Raymond 1954 *Elements Of Social Organization.* Walton & Co. London.
1964 *Essays On Social Organization.* Athlone Press. London.

Franckle, A.H. 1907 *A History of Tibet.* London.

Fraser, J.B. 1829 *Journal Of a Tour Through Part Of The Snowy Ranges Of The Himalaya Mountains And The Sources Of Jumna And Ganges.* London.

Ganguly, J.M. 1971 *Dui Bar* Shri *Kailash Darshan.* East and West Publishers. Calcutta.

Gorger, Geoffrey 1967 Himalayan Village. London.

Goudge, J.E. *Report Of Settlement In the Almora District.* Settlement Report on Parganas Danpur, Askot, Darma, Shor, Kali-Kumaon, Baramandnal, Pali-Pachaun.

Grierson, G.A. 1916 *Linguistic Survey Of India* : Vol. III Part-I. Calcutta.

Haimendorf, Christoph Vo. F. 1975 *Himalayan Traders* : Life in Highland Nepal. John Murray London.

Hardstey, D.L. 1977 *Ecological Anthropology.* John Wiley & Sons. New York.

Harrer, Heinrich 1954 *Seven Years In Tibet.* London.

Hedin, Seven 1906 *Southern Tibet-Discoveries in Former Times Compared To my Own Researches In 1906-08.* London. (12 vols.)

1913 *Trans-Himalaya.* Three Vols. Macmillan London.

Heim, Arnold, and Ganser, August 1937 *The Throne Of The Gods.*

Hill, J. 1963 *Northern India (Himalayas). The Indian Subcontinent.* London.

Hodgsan, B.H. 1847 Notices of the language, literature and religion of the Bauddhas of Nepal and Bhot. Journal of the Asiatic Society of Bengal Part-II, 1235-1246.

Hooker, J.D. 1845 *Himalayan Journal*. London.

Ibbetson, A.W. 1933 *Final Report On The 11th Revenue Settlement Of Garhwal District*. Allahabad.

Joshi, L.D. 1929 *The Khasa Family Law In The Himalayan Districts of the U.P.* Govt. Press. Allahabad.

Kaul, K.K. 1912 *Bhot, Census of India*, 1911. Vol. XIV, Punjab Part-I, Govt. Press, Lahore.

Kaushic, S.D. 1959 *Human Settlement And Occupational Economy In Garhwal-* Bhot Himalayas. Journal of the Asiatic Society of Bengal p. 23-24.

1962 *Climatic Zones And Their Related Social-economy In the Garhwal Himalaya*, Geographical Review of India. XXIV.

1963 *A Geological Study Of The Garhwal And Kumaon Himalayas. Proceedings Of The National Academy Of Sciences*, India. 1965 Vol. XXXV. Section B, Part-IV. p. 25.

Karve, Irawati 1962 *India As a Cultural Region.* Indian Anthropology. Essays in Memory.

Kawaguchi, Eksi 1897-1903 *Three Years In Tibet*. London. Kedarkhand, Chapter 206, Verses

Kluckhon,Clyde 1944 *Navajo Witchcraft*. Papers On The Peaboy Museum Of American Archaeology & Ethnology Clyde.

Lahiri, Atul Chandra 1958 *Kailas Manaser Pathe*. Sign et Press. Calcutta.

Lal, Panna 1911 *An Enquiry Into The Birth And Marriage Customs Of The Khasa And The Bhotias Of Almora Dist.* Indian Antiquary. 46, 190-99.

1942 *Hindu Customary Law In Kumaon*. Govt. Press. Allahabad.

Landor, A. Henry Savage 1898 *In The Forbidden Land*. London.

Louis, J.A.H, 1894 *The Gates Of Tibet*, London.

Maclagen, E.D. 1892 *Bot. Censes of India*, 1891, Vol, XIV : Punjab and its Feudatories, Part-I : Report. Calcutta. p. 295-296.

Martendable Don. 1962 *Social Life And Cultural Change*.

Mason, Kenneth 1955 *Abode Of Snow*. London.

Majumdar, D.N. 1949 *The Social Economy of the Bhotiya*, in K.S. Pangtey, ed Lonely Furrows of the Borderland Folk Culture, Series No. 3 Universal, Lucknow.

Majumdar, D.N. 1961 *Bhotias In Races And Cultures Of India*. Ethnographical Society. Lucknow. p. 272-74.

Mehra, J.D. and Tiwari, S.C. 1955 *The Bhotias Of Almora District*. Vanyajati. 3 (1), 10-16.

Moorcroft, William 1816 *A Journey To Mansarovar In Un-Des, A Province Of Little Tibet*. Asiatic Researches XII, 251-285 : 375-538.

Mumm, A.L.	1909	*Five Months In The Himalayas And Tibet*, London.
Nakane, C. and Prakash, Om.	1964	*Himalay Ke Pahari : Bhotia.* Vanyajati 1964, 13 (1). 25-26.
Oakley, E.S.	1905	*Holy Himalayas*. London.
Oakley, E.S., and Gairola.	1935	*The Himalayan Folklore.* Allahabad.
Ogburn, W.F., & Nimkoff M.F.	1966	*A Handbook of Sociology* Routtedge & Kegan Paul Ltd.
Painuli, Paripuranand	1955	*Sociological Studies of Bhotias.* Vanyajati, 1955, 3 (4), 170-172, Pauri Garhwal Ke Seemavarti Adimjati.
	1956	*Bhotia.* Vanyajati, 1956, 4 (1) 12-13.
	1959	*The Valley Of Gods*. Tehri.
Pandey, Badridatt	1937	*Kumaon Ka Ithas.* Shakti Press. Almora.
Pandey, Hira Vallabh	1950	*Bhotias,* In Tribes of India. Bhartiya Adimjati Sevak Sangh, New Delhi.
Pandey, Mrigesh	1979	*Un Ke Kamgar*. In Nainital Samachar, Feb 15, 1979, Nainital.
Pande T.	1962	*Kumaon Ka Lok Sahitya. Almora* Book Depot. Almora.
Pangtey, K.S.	1948	*The Folk-songs of Bhotias of Kumaon.* Eastern Anthropologist. 1948,7(4),3-9.
Parekh, Navnit	1977	*The Himalayas.* India Book House Pvt. Ltd. Bombay.
Pascoe, E.H.	1964	*A Manual of The Geology of India And Burma.* Vol. II. Calcutta. p. 2026.

Paul, Baden, and C.I.E. B.H.	1974	*The Land Systems of British India*-Vol. II. Oriental Publishers. p. 308-18.
Pauw, E.K.	1896	*Report on The Tenth Settlement of The Garhwal District.*Government Press. Allahabad.
Pranabanand, Swami	1950	*Explorations In Tibet.* Government Press. Allahabad.
	1953	Kailas Mansarovar. Hindi translation published in 1953.
Prasad, Rajeswari	1953	*Census Handbook: Pauri Garhwal,* Government Press. Allahabad.
	1953	Census Handbook: Tehri Garhwal. Government Press Allahabad.
Prasad, R.R.	1979	*Changing Patterns of Transhumant Bhotia Economy.* Man and Nature. Vol. 3, No. 6, November, 1979. Himalayan Seva Sangh. New Delhi.
	1981	*Tribal Stratification in Central Himalayas,* Journal of Social Research, September.
	1981	*A note on Socio-cultural Background of Alcoholism among Jaad Tribals,* Journal of Indian Anthropological Society. 16: 271-273
	1982	*A note on beliefs and practices and pertaining to Child Birth in Bhotia society,* Spectra of Anthropological Progress, 4: 35-37

	1982	*Illness and its Cognitive Aspect among the Jaad Tribals of Central* Himalayas, Social Research, Vo12, Nol. 2, April-June.
	1982	*Obstetrical Practices among the Bhotia Tribals*, Tribal Research Bulletin, Maharashtra State, Pune.
Purohit, Prakas-handra	1978	*Niti Chati*. In, Parvat Piyus.
Rahul, Ram	1970	*The Himalayan Borderland.* Vikas Publication. New Delhi.
Rai, Ramendra Nath	1951	*Kailas O Mansarovar*. Calcutta.
Raipa, Ratan Singh	1975	*Shauka* (in Hindi). Lucknow.
Ram, Pate	1917	*Garhwal: Ancient And Modern*. Army Press. Simla.
Rappaport, Roy. A	1971	*Ritual Sanctity And Cybernetics*. American Anthropologist. 73-76. 73.
Rataudi, Harikrishna	1928	*Garhwal Ka Itihas*. Dehradun.
Rawat, Inder Singh	1971	*Indian Explorers of The 19th Century*. Govt. of India Press. New Delhi.
Rawat Umrawat Singh	1956	*Uttarpath Ki Ek Jhanki*. Lansdown.
Ryan, Bryce F	1969	*Social And Cultural Change*. Ronals Press Company. New York.
Sahlins, Marshall	1964	*Culture And Environment*. The Study of Culural Ecology. In, Sol Tax(Ed.) *Horizons of Anthropology*. Aldinl. Chicago.
Sankritayan, Rahul	1953	*Himalaya Parichay*. Bhag (Part) I: Garhwal. Law Journal Press. Allahabad.

Sanwal, R.D. 1976 *Social Stratification In Rural Kumaon.* Oxford University Press. Delhi.

Sastry, S.S 1975 *The Bhotiya of U.P. Hill Districts* (Central Himalayas), Vanayajati, 23(4).

Sharma, M.M. 1977 *Through The Valley of Gods.* Vision Book. New Delhi.

Sherring, C.A. 1906 *Western Tibet And The British Borderland.* Edward Arnold. London. *Notes on The Bhotias Of Almora And British Garhwal.* Asiatic Society of Bengal. Calcutta.

Sercar, D.C. 1960 *Studies In The Geography of Ancient And Medieval India.* Delhi

Smelser, Neil 1965 *The Sociology of Economic* Life. Prentice Hall of India. New Delhi.

Smith, J.C. 1902 *Settlement Report on Pargana Johar.* Government Press. Allahabad

Sorokin, Pitirim A. 1941 *Social And Cultural Dynamics.* Basic Problems, Principles And Methods. Vol. IV. American Book Company. New York.

Srivastav, S.K. 1949 *Some Problems of Culture Contacts Among The Tharus.* The Eastern Anthropologist. Vol. III. No.1.

1958 *The Tharus: A Study In Cultural Dynamics.* Agra University Press.

Soronsen, S. 1963 *An Index To The Names In The Mahabharata* (Translated by P.C. Roy) Delhi. p. 408.

Spate, O.H.K. 1954 *India And Pakistan*. London. p. 404.

Srivastava, R.P. 1953 *Rangbang In The Changing Bhotia Life*. Eastern Anthropologist, 1953,5,190-203.

1957 *Marriage And Divorce Among The Eastern Bhotias*. The Anthropologist 1957,4,34-43.

1958 *Bhotia Nomads And Their Indo-Tibetan Trade*. Saugar University Journal, 1958,7,1-29.

1966 *Tribe-caste Mobility In India And The Case of The Kumaon Bhotias*. In Haimendorf. Christoph Von Furer (Ed.).

Stowell, V.A 1919 *A Manual of Land Tenures of The Kumaon Division*. Government Press. Allahabad.

Strachey, R. 1851 *On the Physical Geography of the Provinces of Kumaon and Garhwal, in Himalayan Mountains, and of the adjoining part of Tibet*, Journal of Royal Geographical Society: 21.

Thompson, Thomas 1852 *Western Himalayas And Tibet*. London.

Tiwari, S.C. 1952 *The Distribution of Blood Group Among The Bhotias of The Almora District*. Man In India. 1952,32(3) 148-151.

	1954	*Anthropometric Study of Bhotias of Almora District.* The Anthropologist. 1954,1, 22-23.
	1955	*Dermatoglyphics af Bhotias of Almora District* (U.P.). Man In India. 1955,35(2), 94-100.
Trail, George William	1832	*Statistical Report on The Bhotia Mahals of Kumaon.* Asiatic Research, 1832,17,1-50.
Tripathy, R.N.	1973	*Mana-Hamari Sima Ka Ek Gaon.* (Hindi). In Sarhadi Saptahik (Weekly) Ltd. May 19, 1973.
Turner, A.C.	1933	*Bhotiya.* Census of India, 1931, Vol. XVIII: United Provinces of Agra and Oudh, Part-I: Report. Government Press. Allahabad.
Upreti, G.D.	1894	*Proverbs And Folklore of Kūmaon.*
Upreti, H.C.	1968	*The Social Life of The Bhotias.* Vanyajati, 1968,16(1),15-20.
	1965	*Bhotia Dormitory*: A Sociological Analysis. Bulletin of the Tribal Research and Training Institute, Bhopal. 1965,5(1 and 2).
Upreti, R.P.	1967	*The Social Geography of The Bhotias of Uttarkhand.* Studies, The D.S.B. Govt. College, Nainital, Vol. IV, 115-129.
	1968	*Bhotias of Uttarakhand A Study In Anthropogeography. Studies.* Vol. V.p. 115-124.

Vaishnave, Yamunadatt 1974 *Saikron Sal Ke Kumavni Byaparion Ki Romanchak Russ-Yetraen*. Dharma yug. 1974,25 (29). September 15,40,42, New Delhi.

Walton, H.G. 1911 *Gazetteer of The Garhwal District*. Government Press, Allahabad.

1911 *District Gazetteer of The Garhwal District*. Allahabad.

Wedder, T.W. 1902 *The Forests of Upper India And Their Inhabitants*. Edward Arnold. London.

Appendix

APPENDIX I

TABLE—18

Bhotias Population in the Hill Districts of Uttar Pradesh
(Source : Census-1971)

Sl. No.	District	Division	Bhotia Population
1.	Almora	Kumaon	1874
2.	Chamoli	Garhwal	8149
3.	Pithoragarh	Kumaon	14538
4.	Uttarkashi	Garhwal	816
		Total :	25377

TABLE—19

Distribution of Bhotia Population in the Tehsila of Pithoragarh District

Sl.		Bhotia Population		
No.	Tehsil	Total	Male	Female
1.	Dharchula	6738	3482	3256
2.	Didihat	1037	548	489
3.	Munsiari*	6505	3216	3289
4.	Pithoragarh	258	157	101
	Total :	14538	7403	7135

* The Johari Bhotias are concentrated in the Munsiari tehsil of the Pithoragarh District.

APPENDIX No. 2

TABLE SHOWING THE TRADE PARTNERS— Tibetese & JOHARI

Sl. No.	Tibetese Trade Partner	No. of House-holds	Place of Habitation	Different Bhotias Castes/friends of Johar
1	2	3	4	5
1.	Singkor	325	Singkorthol	Nikhurpa, Mapkara, Pangti, Dharamskatu
2.	Garche	150	Garchethol	Tolia
3.	Garge	140	Gargethol	Mapkara, Dhamsaktu
4.	Phingchi	45	——	Jangpangi
5.	Seliphuk	30	——	Pangti, Dhamsaktu, Mertolia
6.	Pangrang	35	Pangrangthol	Pangti
7.	Dhukgang	20	Horgungu	Pangti
8.	Derfu, Ju	45	Dijithol	Ghangharia, Sayana
9.	Lundru	30	——	Mertolia, Rawat
10.	Bungbuwa	210	Bunghoj	Biljwal, Mertolia, Rawat
11.	Dongpal	15	Dongpu	Pangti
12.	Khinglungi	45	Khinglung	Pangti, Dhamsaktu
13.	Dama	35	Dama	Pangti
14.	Kelakapa	17	Kelak	Pangti, Mertolia
15.	Misraba	50	Miser	Pangti, Jangbangi

1	2	3	4	5
16.	Dunchu	32	Dunchuthol	Jungbangi, Mertolia, Rawat
17.	Chujia	10	Chuthol	Pangti
18.	Gajkapa	38	Darchin	Pangti
19.	Korpan	60	Korpanthol	Rawat, Jangbangi, Tolia
20.	Jungbuba	35	Jungbubathol	Sayana
21.	Chachuwa	40	Chachuthol	Rawat
22.	Langchu	44	Langchuthol	Burfal
23.	Sarleba	50	Soakthol	Jangbangi, Pangti, Biljwal
24.	Bheri Bungbuwa	80	——	Pangti, Panchpal
25.	Horgeba	8	——	Tolia, Biljwal
26.	Majen	32	——	Dongspa, Tolia, Ghangharia
27.	Nabru	—	——	Mapkara

TRUE COPY

APPENDIX III

आड़ती (मित्रिया डंक) के नियम

1. आज के तारीण से जो कोई भी नया आड़ती तिब्बतियों के साथ बजरिये गमग्या (नियम पत्र) लगायेगा, उसको लाजिम होगा कि एक साल के भीतर वह बृटिश देश ऐजेन्ट गर्तोक की अदालत में रजिस्ट्री करा के उनकी मनजुरी देने से पहिले पूरी तहकीकात करेगी।

2. जो कोई भी अपना आड़ती हक (तिब्बतियो के साथ) वे पे या दूसरे का हक छारी देगा, उनको लाजिम है कि ऐसी लिखत पड़त सरकारी स्टाम्प पर करे ओर ऐसी खरीद फरोख्त गर्तोक को सूचना देनी चाहिये।

3. अगर कोई आदमी किसी दूसरे के आड़त के आथ तिब्बत में या हिन्दोस्तान में जालसाजी, जबरदस्ती या बिना हक के व्यापार करेगा, उसको 100/- एक सौ रुपया, जुर्माना होगा। लेकिन अगर यह यह साबित कर देगा कि भूल से ऐसा व्यापार किया गया है तो अदालत जुर्मानाने के बाबजूद विचार करेगी।

4. अगर किसी तिब्बती आड़त का लड़का या लड़की दूसरे तिब्बती के घर दामाद या शादी में दिया जायगा तो जिस घर में जाये उस घर के ही आड़त का पूरा हक होगा और माँ-बाप के आड़त का कोई हक नहीं रहेगा चाहे लड़का या लड़की अपने साथ कितना ही माल या भेड़ बकरी वगेरह ले जावे।

5. अगर किसी का आड़त अपना गाँव छोड़कर दूसरे "दे" या इलाका या गाँव में जाकर बस जाये या ठलया (रय्यत) हो जाये तो पुराने आड़त का ही हक समझा जायेगा। अगर कोई बिना आड़त वाला तिब्बती इस तरह किसी "दे" या इलाके में बस जाये, ओर ठलवा (रय्यत) हो वावे तो "दे" आड़त वाले का ही हक रहेगा, और दूसरा आदमी उसके साथ आड़त नहीं लग सकेगा।

6. सबसे, आइन्दा आड़ती बावत जिसका दावा झूठा निकलेगा उस पर एक सौ रुपये का जुर्माना किया जायगा। इस जुर्माने का आधा याने पचास रुपया मुदलि को दिये जायेंगे और बाकी पचास रुपये सरकारी खजाना में जमा होगे।

7. प्रत्येक आदमी को इस बात का विशेष सावधानी रखनी पड़ेगी कि वह अपने आड़ती के मय कुटुम्ब के नाम याद रखें।

8. मित्रताई का दावा ऐजेन्सी अदालत में जहाँ तक हो सके किया जाये।

9. जब कोई दूसरे के आड़त को कर्जा देगा तो वह सिर्फ अपने रुपयों की वसूली का ही हकदार रहेगा और नमक, सोहागा, ओर ऊन पर उनका का कोई हक नहीं होगा।

मुकाम ज्ञानिमा तिब्बत,	British Trade Agent
ता० 14, अगस्त 1945	GARTOK

APPENDIX IV

TABLE—20

Memo of Imports Purchased from the Bhotias between October 1840 and May 1841 Johar Pass

Description of Goods	Quantity (Mds)	Value (Rs.)	Rate at which sold
1	2	3	4
Tincal, or unrefined barad	9,000	45,000	The present rate is Rs. 5/- per md.
Salt	2,000	8,000	Sold at Rs. 4/- per md. and bartered for rice in the proportion of 3 or 4 seers of grain for one seer of salt.
Chouris	10	1,600	3 to 8 Rupees per seer
Zedoary Nirbisi	2	250	1-8 to 5 Rupees per seer
Saffron	1	500	8 to 12 Rupees per seer
Tea	2	200	2-8 to 4 Rupees per seer
Psham or shawl wool	15	750	30 to 70 Rupees per maund
Ponies	60	3,000	30 to 150 Rupees each
Shawls	40 pairs	1,500	20 to 60 Rupees per pair
Chinese dragon & Silk	20 pieces	1,200	100 to 125 Rupees per piece, and plain kind from 6 to 15 Rupees each piece

1	2	3	4
Blankets, clothing, coarse woollen and serges	500 pieces	2,000	2 to 12 Rupees per piece
Goats and sheep	1,000	1,2000	1 to 12 Rs. each
Mule-Yaks (Jubcos)	50	1,000	20 to 30 Rs. each
Musk	80 Tolas	200	1 to 8 to 3 Rupees per tola
Gold Dust	1500 Petanas	1,200	8 Rupees per Petang
Ladakh tunnashas, or 3 anna pieces	——	7,000	Exchange at 4×5 per Rupees
Kuldar Rupees	——	15,000	The sale cash return in India coinage
Total Rupees:		1,00,400	

TABLE—21

Memo of Goods Exported from Almora to Chinese Tartary between October 1840 and May 1847 (Johar Pass)

Description of Goods	Quantity (mds).	Value (Rupees)
Sugarcandy	70 mands	2,000
Gur	5,000 bhelees	1,000
Confectionary	20 mands	400
Dates	70—do—	1,300
Almond	25—do—	700
Cloves	3—do—	400
Nutmegs	2—do—	100
Cardamoms	3—do—	500
Camphor	1—do—	225
Indigo	2—do—	500
Pewters and Sal almonds	5—do—	150
Khin Khabs	2—do—	300
Broad Clothes	175 pieces	17,000
Moleskin & other	175—do—	4,000
European clothes	175—do—	4,000
Kharwa	4,000—do—	3,000
Coarse Clothes	11,000—do—	13,000
Pearls	...	1,500
Coral	...	800
Misc. commodities as penkinives' buttons, & chinaware	...	55
		12,000
Hardware	......	1,000
Tobacco	200 mds	2,000
Betelnut	5 mds	200
	Total Rs. :	62,875

TABLE—22

Rough Explanation of differences according to the Papers given in by a Principal native Merchant of Almora

Expense as follows	*Rupees*
Sheep & Goats purchased for carriage	10,000
Cotton clothes purchased for apparel	4,000
Coarse Tibetan woollens re-purchased for apparel	4,000
Government land revenue	4,849
Interest of loans from Almora merchants	15,000
Expenses for juboos, goats and sheep for domestic use	4,000
Loans advanced by Bhotias	4,000
Losses of au kinds	6,000
Total ;	51,849
Profit balance in favour of Bhotias	24,476
Difference between exports and imports	76,325

TABLE—23

Memo. of goods sold to the Bhotias of the Johar Pass by Merchants of Almora and other Traders from 15th May to 15th June, 1841 at Munsiari, according to a rough Native calculation, made in the Settlement Camps of J. H. Batten Esq.

	Rupees
Broadcloth	4,000
Moleskin	800
Stin jean	300
American Drill	50

English Chintz	300
English Calicoes, muslin, linen etc.	1,000
Velvet	400
Indian Chintz, Calicoes etc.	4,700
Pearls	700
Coral	400
Indigo	350
Spices	160
Sugar	250
Delhi valuables, precious stone, Jewellery, curroitees ets.	500
Total :	14,210

Brought For Sale By Zamindars

Grain	60
Tobacco and oil	200
Grand Total * :	15,010

* In one month at one place viz. Munsiari, half way between Bageshwar and Millam.

TABLE – 24

Item of Export – 1922 (in maunds –).

Sl. No.	Item	Export from Jangla	Bampa	Dharechula	Lilam
1.	Foreign Cloth	—	79	44	166
5.	Indian Cloth	6	49	257	516
3.	Grain & Pulse	—	1740	115	—
4.	Whet	88	113	1859	1468
5.	Rice	834	1226	6217	1355
6.	Other Grains	—	314	644	—
7.	Sugar	—	—	34	31
8.	Gur	—	—	3977	300
9.	Tea	—	—	81	10
10.	Tobacco	2	43	246	23
11.	Silver	1900	25140	58163	19700

TABLE—25

Items of Import 1922—In Maunds

Sl. No.	Item	Imported from Tibet in			
		Jangla	Bampa	Dharechula	Lilam
1.	Borax	—	2874	12167	13793
2.	Salt	776	10889	1817	8733
3.	Wool	192	2427	5414	3748
4.	Woollen Clothes	6	75	448	15

TABLE–26

Import of Animals (1922)

Sl. No.	Animal	brought from Tibet in			
		Jangla	Dampa	Dharechula	Lilam
1.	Horse	2	50	37	166
2.	Jaaboo	—	70	23	54
3.	Goat & Sheep	905	13138	5958	—
4.	Other Animals	—	40	—	—

TABLE—27

	Export & Imports			Export	Imports
	Rs.	Rs.		Rs.	Rs.
1877-78	94,924	3,09,507	1880-81	1,46,882	3,84,170
1878-79	1,13,016	2,39,073	1881-82	1,88,660	3,92,302
1879-80	1,64,880	3,26,259	1882-83	1,94,303	3,43,932

TABLE—28

Export of Cotton Cloth By Bhotias

	Weight Mds.	Value Rs.		Weight Mds.	Value Rs.
1877-78	305	12,674	1880-81	438	23,889
1878-79	262	18,455	1881-82	462	24,823
1879-80	417	19,409	1882-83	496	28,750

TABLE—29

Export of Grains By the Bhotias

	Weight Mds.	Value Rs.		Weight Mds.	Value Rs.
1877-78	28,116	49,151	1880-81	43,330	97,334
1878-79	34,646	74,276	1881-82	46,796	1,18,584
1879-80	39,289	1,16,919	1882-83	62,416	1,35,870

TABLE—30

Export of Sugar & C. By the Bhotias

	Weight Mds.	Value Rs.		Weight Mds.	Value Rs
1877-78	7,561	23,068	1880-81	3,437	19,818
1878-79	1,868	12,067	1881-82	5,559	42,410
1879-80	5,178	23,437	1882-83	3,814	23,954

TABLE—31

Import of Borax From Tibet By Bhotias

	Weight Mds.	Value Rs.		Weight Mds.	Value Rs.
1877-78	22,694	71,433	1880-81	28,536	1,70,730
1878-79	18,544	92,799	1881-82	33,821	1,02,926
1879-80	18,948	94,616	1882-83	51,527	1,72,216

TABLE—32

Import of Salt from Tibet By the Bhotias

	Weight Mds.	Value Rs.		Weight Mds.	Value Rs.
1877—78	31,709	1,09,072	1880-81	37,531	1,55,790
1978—79	21,453	81,754	1881-82	27,717	1,10,868
1879—80	39,785	1,81,681	1882-83	34,946	1,39,784

TABLE—33

Import of Wool & C From Tibet By the Bhotias

	Raw	Manufactured	Value Rs.		Raw Manufactured	Value Rs.
1877-78	6,225	1,072	1,09,845	1880-81	2,985	59,936
1878-79	2,049	255	54,143	1881-82	2,912	77,081
1879-80	2,373	311	51,275	1882-83	2,266	49,363

*The Source of all these tables are the Himalayan Gazetteer, By E.T. Atkinson, Vol. III, Cosmo Publications, 1973, p. 135-39.

APPENDIX – V

TABLE—34

Occupational Categories In 16 Bhotia Villages

Sl. no.	Bhotia Village	Total No. of families	Nature of occupation	OCCUPATIONS OF BHOTIAS: Agriculture	Wool Work	Service	Sheep Rearing	Shop Keeping	Contract labour	Casual labour	Other
1	2	3	4	5	6	7	8	9	10	11	12
1.	Talla Dummer	30	Main	7(23.23%)	11(36.67%)	3(10%)	5(16.67%)	1(3.33%)	1(3.33%)	2(6.67%)	— —
			Subsidiary	1(3.33%)	7(23.33%)	15(50%)	1(3.33%)	—	—	1(3.39%)	3(10%)
2.	Mal la Dummer	19	Main	4(21.05%)	4(21.05)	3(15.79%)	4(21.05%)	—	1(5.26%)	2(10.53%)	1(5.26%)
			Subsidiary	6(31.59%)	8(42.11)	1(5.26%)	3(15.79%)	— —	2(10.53%)	—	—
3.	Tejam	23	Main	15(65.22%)	2(8.90%)	2(8.70%)	—	4(17.39%)	—	—	—
			Subs.	4(17.39%)	15(65.22%)	1(4.35%)	—	3(13.64%)	—	—	—
4.	Timtia	11	Main	1(9.09%)	5(21.74%)	4(17.39%)	—	1(9.09%)	—	—	—
			Subs.	6(26.09%)	3(27.27%)	1(0.89%)	—	—	—	—	—
5.	Darkot	40	Main	14(35.00%)	24(42.25%)	8(20.00%)	(10%)	7(17.5 %)	—	—	—
			Subs.	28(70.00%)	6(10.00%)	—	(7.5%)	—	—	—	—
6.	Daranthi	8	Main	1(12.50%)	3(37.50%)	2(25.00%)	—	2(25.00%)	—	—	—
			Subs.	7(87.50%)	4(50.00%)	—	—	—	—	—	—

1	2	3	4	5	6	7	8	9	10	11	12
7.	Ranthi	6	Main	1(16.67%)	3(50.00%)	—	—	2(33.33%)	—	—	—
			Subs.	3(50.00%)	1(16.67%)	—	—	—	—	—	—
8.	Mapwalwada	7	Main	1(14.29%)	4(57.14%)	—	—	2(33.33%)	—	—	—
			Subs.	4(57.14%)	2(33.33%)	—	—	1(14.29%)	—	—	—
9.	Thal	20	Main	3(15.00%)	4(20%)	2(10.00%)	—	13(65.00%)	2(10.00%)	—	—
			Subs.	7(35.00%)	9(45.00%)	9(45.00%)	—	—	—	—	—
10.	Bageshwar	9	Main	1(11.11%)	2(22.22%)	1(11.11%)	—	4(44.44%)	1(11.11%)	—	—
			Subs.	—	4(44.44%)	1(11.11%)	—	—	—	—	—
11.	Garur	12	Main	—	1(8.33%)	1(8.33%)	—	7(66.69%)	2(16.67%)	—	—
			Subs.	—	5(41.67%)	—	—	—	4(33.33%)	—	—
12.	Didihat	16	Main	—	1(8.33%)	1(8.33%)	2(12.5%)	12(75.00%)	—	—	—
			Subs,	—	5(31.65%)	—	2(12.5%)	1(8.33%)	—	—	—
13.	Almora	4	Main	—	—	1(25.00%)	—	3(75.00%)	—	—	—
			Subs.	—	2(50.00%)	—	—	—	—	—	—
14.	Gwaldham	5	Main	—	—	—	—	5(1000.00%)	—	—	—
			Subs.	—	3(60.00%)	—	—	—	—	—	—
15.	Haldwani	12	Main	—	—	6(50.00%)	—	5(41.67%)	1(8.33%)	—	—
			Subs.	—	4(33.33%)	—	—	—	—	—	—
16.	Pithoragarh	2	Main	—	—	—	—	2(100.00%)	—	—	—
			Subs.	—	2(100.00%)	—	—	—	—	—	—
	Total	224	Main	48(21.42)	44(15.18%)	34(15.18%)	15(6.69%)	70(31.25%)	8(3.57%)	4(1.79%)	1(.45%)
			Subsidiary	66(29.46%)	70(31.25%	19(8.48%)	9(4.02%)	5(2.23%)	6(2.68%)	1(.45%)	3(1.34%)

APPENDEX —VI

Kumaon and Uttarakhand Zamindari Abolition and Land Reforms Act. 1960

(U.P. Act No. XVII of 1960)

AN

ACT

to provide for the acquisition of the rights, title and interests of persons between the State and the tiller of the soil in certain areas of the Kumaon Division and in Uttarakhand Division and for the introduction of land reforms therein.

Whereas it is expedient to provide for the acquisition of the rights, title and interest of the persons between the State and the tiller of the soil in certain areas of the Kumaon Division and in Uttarakhand Division and for the introduction of land reforms therein ;

It is hereby enacted as follows in the Eleventh year of the Republic of India.

CHAPTER-II

10.

Every person who, on the date immediately preceeding to the appointed date, was

(a) a *Sirtan* holding from a *hissedar* : or

(b) a Sirtan holding from a *Khaikar* ; or

(c) a mortgagee in actual possession of land mentioned in a section 8 ; or

(d) a lessee of the rights of a hissedar in non-Khaikhar land and a lessee or sub-lessee mentioned in section 34 or the Tehri Garhwal Bhumi-Sambandh ; Adhikari Niyams, 1941, of the rights of a khaikar or those of a maurusidar in non-khaikhar land having any land in his personal cultivation as such ; or

(e) recorded as occupant of land held by a hissedar or a khaikhar as such in the last revision of records made under Chapter IV of the U.P. land Revenue Act, 1901 ;

Shall be called *asami* of the land and shal!, subject to the provision of this Act, be entitled to take or reta in possession thereof.

12.

Every *hissedar* whose rights, title, or interest are acquired under Section 4, shall be entitled to receive and be paid compensation as hereinafter provided.

19.

(i) The compensations payable to a *hissedar* under section 12 shall be thirty times of the amount arrived at after deducting the land revenue payable both by the *hissedar* in respect of his khaikari land from its rental income referred to in section 18.

APPENDIX —II
TABLE—35
Family Type in the 16 Bhotia Villages

Sl. No.	Bhotia Village	Total No. of families	Family Type: Nuclear No./%	Joint No./%	Extended No./%	Single person household No./%
(1)	(2)	(3)	(4)	(5)	(6)	(7)
1.	Talla Dummer	30	19 (63.33)	8 (26.66)	2 (6.66)	1 (3.33)
2.	Malla Dummer	19	8 (42.18)	9 (47.36)	1 (5.26)	1 (5.26)
3.	Tejam	23	15 (65.21)	6 (26.08)	1 (4.34)	1 (4.34)
4.	Timtia	11	7 (63.63)	1 (0.09)	3 (27.27)	- -
5.	Darkot	40	24 (60.00)	14 (35.00)	2 (5.00)	- -
6.	Daranthi	8	6 (75.00)	2 (25.00)	- -	- -
7.	Mapwalwada	7	4 (57.14)	2 (28.57)	1 (14.29)	- -
8.	Thal	20	15 (75.00)	5 (25.00)	- -	- -
9.	Bageshwar	9	7 (77.77)	2 (22.22)	- -	- -
10.	Garur	12	9 (75.00)	3 (25.00)	- -	- -
11.	Didihat	16	12 (75.00)	4 (25.00)	- -	- -
12.	Almora	4	3 (75.00)	1 (25.00)	- -	- -
13.	Gwaldham	5	3 (60.00)	2 (40.00)	- -	- -
14.	Haldwani	18	7 (58.33)	3 (25.00)	2 (16.67)	- -
15.	Pithoragarh	2	- -	- -	2 (100.00)	- -
16.	Ranthi	6	4 (66.70)	2 (33.30)	- -	- -
	Total	224	143 (63.84)	64 (28.57)	14 (6.25)	3 (1.34)

Glossary of Terms

Term	
Asan	Prayer-rug
Ekhkhu	Woollen overcoat
Bhabhar	Himalayan Foothills
Bheli	Weight which measures approximately 750 gms.
Bhoot-Pitra-Chechet	Rituals Concerned with the Ancestor worship
Bukcha	Woollen Boot
Bugyal	Alpine Pasture
Burrah	Village Headman
Chakti	Germented Liquor of Bhotias
Chatni	Sauce
Chutka	Thick Coarse Woollen Rug
Dann	Woollen Carpet
Des	Country
Duk	Tibetan Dragon
Doka	Basket Made of Bamboo
Furu	A Wooden Bowl
Gamgia	Written Trade Agreement
Ghar—Pradhan	Resident Landlord
Hissedar	Original Proprietor of Land and the Cultivator

Term	
Jibu	Yak
Kamin	Headman
Karbas	Saddlebag
Katwa	Hand Spindle
Khaikar	Khaikars are those people who cultivate lands in his village owned by people of other village and are the Hissedars.
Khampa	A Tibetan Tribe
Mandi	Mart
Malla	Upper Region
Nali	240 sq. yards make 1 Nali
Nangri	People of Lower Region
Nyay-Panchyat	The Institution of Judiciary at the village level
Padhan	Village Headman
Pagra	A Piece of White Cloth which tied round the woman's waist.
Pahari	People Inhabiting the Hilly Tract of Kumaon Regions.
Sirtan	Tenant Cultivator
Talla	Lower Region
Tehsil	Administrative Sub-division of a District in Uttar Pradesh
Terai	Regions of Himalayan Foothill.
That	Right in Land
Thatwan	Proprietor of land
Thulma	Thick Woollen Blanket
Zimidar	The Tiller of Land.

Index

Illustrations

Fig. 1 Wool spinning—a favourite pastime of the Bhotias

Fig. 2 Bhotia males.

Fig. 3 Terraced fields of the Bhotia region.

Fig. 4 A view of a Bhotia village.

Fig. 5 A Bhotia woman on her loom.

Fig. 6 'Dann'—woollen carpet of the Bhotias.

Fig. 7 Subsistence farming.

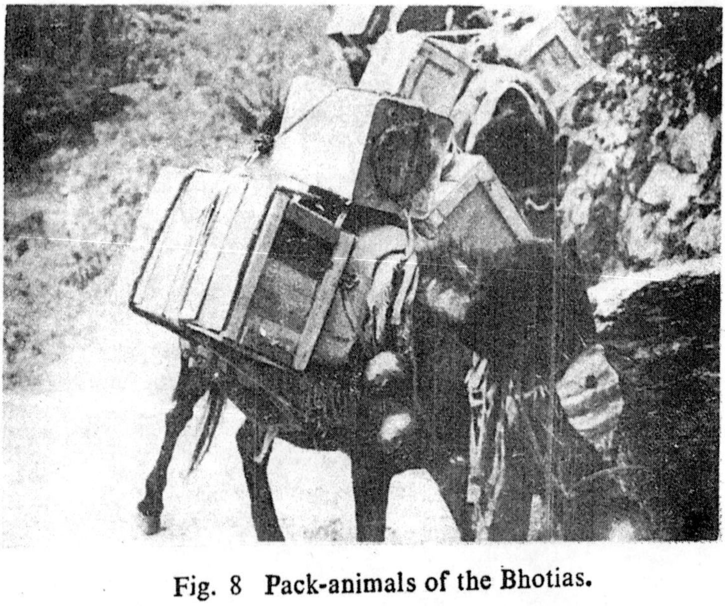

Fig. 8 Pack-animals of the Bhotias.